CHRISTMAS WITH MARY ENGELBREIT

HERE COMES SANTA CLAUS

Illustrated by
MARY
ENGELBREIT

Photography by
JOHN GOULD BESSLER

Written by
VITTA POPLAR

Andrews McMeel
Publishing

Kansas City

Christmas with Mary Engelbreit: Here Comes Santa Claus
© 2002 by Mary Engelbreit Ink.

Published simultaneously by Andrews McMeel Publishing and
Oxmoor House, Inc.

www.andrewsmcmeel.com
www.maryengelbreit.com

 and Mary Engelbreit are registered trademarks of Mary Engelbreit Enterprises, Inc.

Library of Congress Cataloging-in-Publication Data
Engelbreit, Mary.
    Christmas with Mary Engelbreit : here comes Santa Claus.
      p. cm.
    ISBN: 0-7407-2538-6
     1. Christmas decorations. 2. Christmas cookery. I. Title: Here comes Santa Claus. II.
    Title

    TT900.C4 E52 2002
    745.594'12—dc21   20022018678

First U.S. Edition
02 03 04 05 06 MHN 10 9 8 7 6 5 4 3 2 1

Produced by Smallwood & Stewart, Inc., New York City
Designer: Amy Henderson
Stylist: Lori Hellander
Recipe developer: Sarah Zwiebach

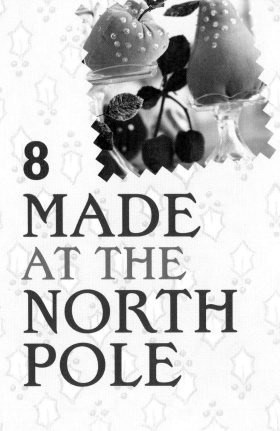

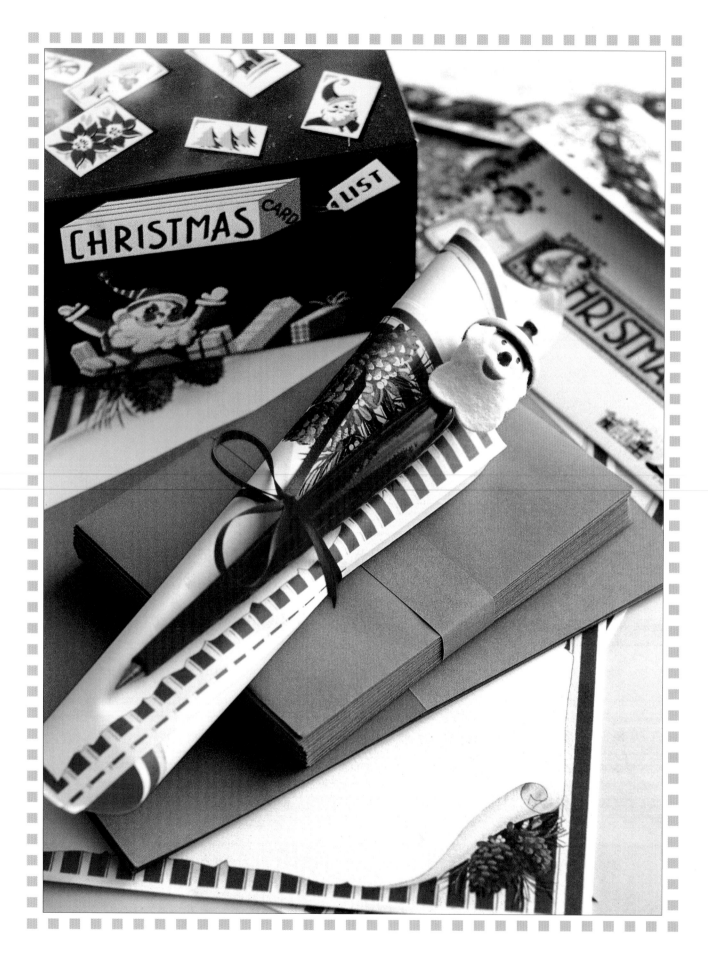

Please join us...

Trim a trellis? Bake a village? Sew a mouse? This is not your ordinary Christmas book—we created this one to help you plan every holiday element, even how to write the best letters to Santa.

We make jillions of homemade projects that anyone can do—really. And we jumpstart your holiday parties with recipes and "scripts" for gatherings that break the mold, from a family picnic on the porch to a treasure hunt for friends. Create an unexpected and memorable Christmas while staying sane. Sound good? Then read on.

Mary

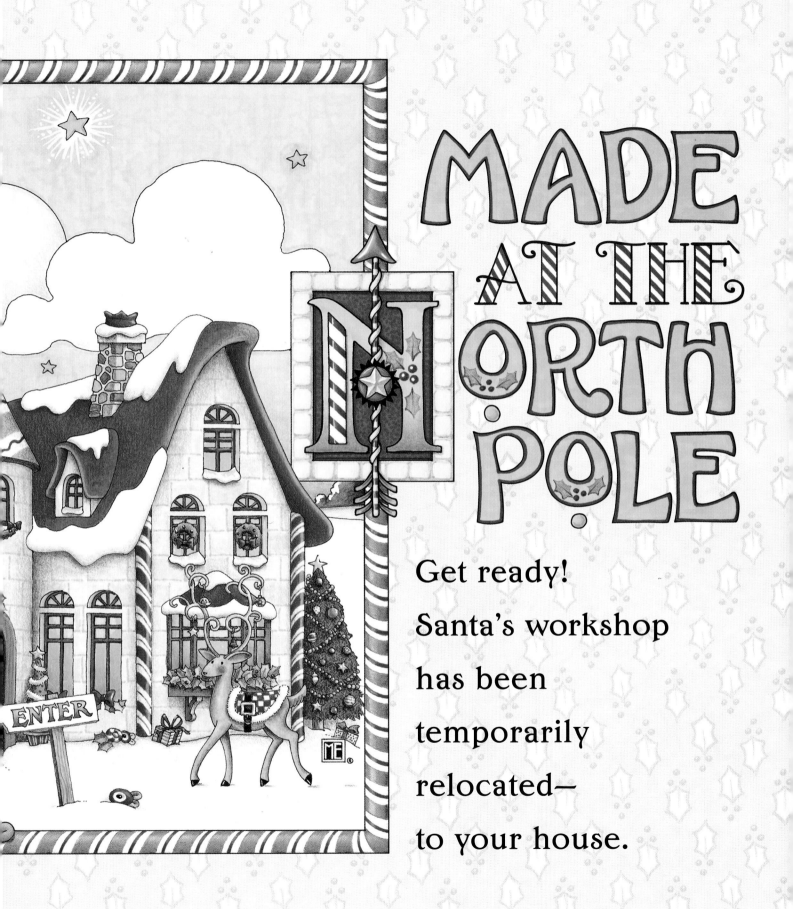

MADE AT THE NORTH POLE

Get ready!
Santa's workshop
has been
temporarily
relocated—
to your house.

nyone can head to the store and walk away with a blouse or the latest electronic device. These sorts of presents are certainly appreciated, but they are rarely cherished. Instead, it's the little gift, made by hand with love and thoughtfulness, that we remember for years to come. When you craft an object or bake cookies for someone, you're actually offering a bit of yourself. And the homemade gift is available to everyone, even—especially—the most budget-minded.

Making gifts at home is a powerful antidote to an insatiable appetite for presents, the syndrome that often affects children at holidays. Kids actively involved in the gift-making process will focus less on their own wish lists.

Creating presents for others fosters a keener appreciation of the gifts they'll be receiving, too.

Homemade presents needn't be something you can hold in your hand, however. You might offer your talents. If you're handy, help paint a friend's apartment. Make an unexpected phone call or write a chatty letter. Best of all, create a memory for a child unique to this year—perhaps an ice skating expedition to the local pond. It's not about money. It's about giving.

SCOOP UP SOME FRUITS

Previous page: This year, sew up a fruit salad of puffy velvet ornaments. Fill up candy jars of them as we've done, and draw handmade labels. Larger-than-life cherries swinging from vintage pipe cleaners and irresistibly ripe apples and pears are glamorous keepsakes that will be holiday reminders through the dreary months of winter. WORKSHOP PAGE 117

LET'S TRIM THE TRELLIS

With a fresh coat of paint, a garden trellis becomes the perfect prop for posting holiday cards and Christmas notes. Attach them with wooden clothespins that have been painted in a bright contrasting color. If you don't have a trellis, get a section of lattice at the lumber yard and paint it any color you want.

A CANINE CHRISTMAS

Now fabric can be customized through the modern magic of photo transfer. A pillow to honor the dog lover features images from both vintage Christmas cards and wallpaper. For a real shortcut, go to a copy center, where they can duplicate your color image onto waxy transfer paper that can be ironed onto fabric. A few tips: If you want to work with family photos, by all means do, but go for those that are relatively stark, without too much background detail. The photo transfer process works best when the image is colorful and graphic. Shiny poplin fabric is best for photo transfer because its sheen shows off the image well. ❄ WORKSHOP **PAGE 118**

BIOGRAPHY IN A BOX

Imagine telling the story of someone's life in ten objects or less. When you frame signature pieces and everyday objects in a shadowbox, you sketch a memorable portrait in a unique way. That's Mary's own shadowbox on top, complete with her trademark glasses, art supplies, and treasured scottie motif. The box at bottom left tells the tale of a world traveler, while the box by its side is a time capsule of a favorite uncle's possessions. Simply collage items with archival glue or rest them on the frame itself.

YOU WERE SEW GOOD THIS YEAR

Though we see them everywhere, cell phones have a way of disappearing if you don't keep constant tabs on them. With this in mind, we present the handmade cell phone holder, worn fashionably over the shoulder or on a belt loop. We've whipped ours up in two different fabrics: a serene toile with a tassel closure for the sophisticates among us and a sparkly denim for the younger set. Don't feel hemmed in by our fabric choices. You can personalize the holder, selecting perhaps a snappy stripe for your teenage son or a hunting print for Uncle Joe. ❊ WORKSHOP PAGE 118

After all that work, you deserve a gift for yourself, don't you think? A sewing box will help keep supplies organized and in pristine condition. These creations—which, incidentally, make fabulous gifts as well—began with bandboxes that were painted with solid colors and freehand stripes. For the trimmings, we chose a tape measure, various cloth ribbons, and favorite vintage buttons. The labels are lettered with a paint pen. You could also photocopy old sewing patterns to découpage to the boxes.

Material Gifts

A bit of fabric and yarn comes in handy at the holidays. Vintage sweaters can be crafted into sweaters for dogs, caps for kids, and catnip pillow covers for the kitties. Color-copy fabric onto paper for trompe l'oeil projects—for instance, copy a hand-knitted sweater and découpage the image onto a bed tray. Sew a remnant into a sack to carry an oddly shaped gift. The ancient Japanese art of wrapping and knotting fabric around gift boxes is called "furoshiki." When you do it, create layers of contrasts like organza with tulle netting; cinch the fabrics with wired ribbon.

I want it all

Writing Successful Letters to Santa

We'll Play: Kids and grown-ups alike get together to write Christmas lists that are sure to get Santa's attention!

We'll Feast: For inspiration, serve luscious baked brie, tea sandwiches, the creamiest potato soup, and fabulous reindeer cookies.

Does Santa know what you want? Never take for granted that he does. The very best way to be sure is to say it in a letter. And when a group gets together to share letter-writing, it's even more fun. This is a party for kids, but the adults can also take the opportunity to put their thoughts into writing... you never know who might actually read your letter!

You will need some art supplies for this occasion. Outfit a children's table with plenty of letter-writing goodies. Ruled notebook paper or even a large roll of

VERY, VERY GOOD—HONEST

Encourage good penmanship by tacking up Christmas stationery with notes to Santa. Crayons, felt-tip pens, even pencils all get his attention, so have a dictionary on hand to check spelling. Cheery surroundings inspire letter writers: Toss out a special canvas welcome mat for Santa and your guests; decorate plain white lampshades with jolly holiday cutouts. WORKSHOP PAGES 119, 121

COUNTING THE DAYS

A jacob's ladder calendar, held together by strips of narrow ribbon, is a stacking structure that features illustrations from long ago. As surprising as an advent calendar, it reveals itself month by month through the year and is vastly entertaining. Rather than vintage illustrations, you could choose kids' artwork or appropriate family photos for each month. WORKSHOP PAGE 120

plain white butcher paper that can be torn into pieces will do. A cache of stickers and stamps is also handy. Some children feel most comfortable using crayons; others will want to try their hands at fountain pens and colored inks. For those who really want to get Santa's attention, offer safety scissors and construction paper for

cutouts, sponges to stamp shapes with poster paint, and even photographs of themselves that they can attach to the cards. Convert a tissue box into a mailbox by covering it with gift wrap. As a bonus, you get the cards as keepsakes.

Since this is a party that's all about Santa, he deserves to inspire the decorating motif. Let his cheery smile beam from vintage holiday postcards and other paper memorabilia around the rooms; display your collectible Santa teapots, cookie jars, and snow globes. Serve kid-friendly food that can be made ahead—simple sandwiches, hearty soup, a warm baked brie, an assortment of crackers, and some crunchy apple slices. By all means, offer guests fantastic Christmas cookies, plates and plates of them. Santa is sure to know you've been very, very good, all year.

Step right up and **tell Santa** what you **really want.**

WAIT A MINUTE, MR. POSTMAN

Kids' creativity can be jump-started with writing utensils. A Santa, snowman, or candy-cane pen will get the ballpoint rolling. Package each child's letter supplies together like a gift, wrapped with ribbon. Encourage kids to ask not just for themselves, but to think of others, too. Hang their finished notes around the room with decorated push pins.

A BUFFET SURE TO LURE SANTA INDOORS

Where is it written that Christmas gatherings must feature elaborate, painstakingly prepared foods that require a culinary degree? We say humbug to that. The object is for family and friends to mingle and chat, snack and sip, without the fear that they've got the wrong knife to butter the bread. Dress up basic foods by presenting them with panache and they somehow transcend their humble origins. Spinach soup arrives in a steamy tureen, tiny sandwiches—even some peanut butter and jelly ones—are poised on a pedestal, and a small brie, baked and drenched with store-bought praline-mustard glaze, is slipped into a cozy ramekin and served with crackers. Even the apples rest under sparkling glass domes.
PANTRY **PAGES 95-97**

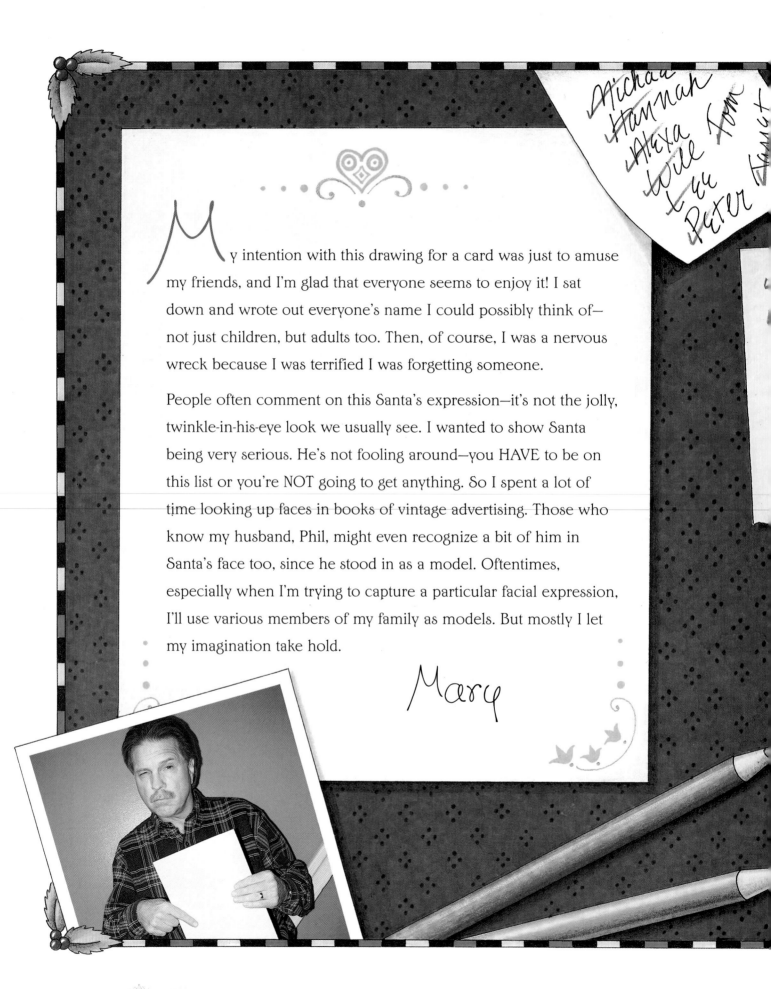

My intention with this drawing for a card was just to amuse my friends, and I'm glad that everyone seems to enjoy it! I sat down and wrote out everyone's name I could possibly think of—not just children, but adults too. Then, of course, I was a nervous wreck because I was terrified I was forgetting someone.

People often comment on this Santa's expression—it's not the jolly, twinkle-in-his-eye look we usually see. I wanted to show Santa being very serious. He's not fooling around—you HAVE to be on this list or you're NOT going to get anything. So I spent a lot of time looking up faces in books of vintage advertising. Those who know my husband, Phil, might even recognize a bit of him in Santa's face too, since he stood in as a model. Oftentimes, especially when I'm trying to capture a particular facial expression, I'll use various members of my family as models. But mostly I let my imagination take hold.

Mary

FOR GOODNESS SAKE

If you're serious about Christmas, you know it's essential to make sure Santa feels really welcome. Don't wait until the last minute to get ready for this important visit! Plan wisely and well and you will be rewarded. Santa may even skip a house or two when he detects the irresistible aroma of just-baked anise cookies wafting from your oven. The distinctive flavor of this recipe is a nice variation on milder sugar cookies, and it is versatile enough to mold into endless shapes. Teddy bears, Santa's boots, reindeer, wooden soldiers, snowmen, gingerbread boys and girls, candles, and Christmas trees... there are so many designs. Anise cookies take decorations—jam, melted chocolate, chopped nuts, and of course, brightly tinted frosting—wonderfully too. Pack some up in paper bags for Santa to take along on the rest of his journey. Just to be totally sure you've enchanted Santa, set out a batch of peanut butter fudge he can slip into his right pocket and peanut brittle for his left one. Both are easy to make and deliver a sugary burst of energy. ❄ **PANTRY PAGE 97-98**

Presentation Is All

An old school lunchbox packed with homemade cookies; a vintage gathering basket nestling pungent cheese straws— these imaginative containers make food gifts especially fun. Scout around for jelly molds and cake tins that can be dressed with tulle and ribbon to hold holiday treats. Spruce up old glass jars with strips of rickrack. Simplest of all is a plain paper bag; glue on a vintage postcard or recycled Christmas card, add a polka dot bow, and fill it with treats.

ON CHRISTMAS DAY
IN THE MORNING

Present Mom—or your sister or your favorite aunt—with a neckroll and a selection of eye-opening treats. Wrap fabric around a roll of quilt batting or a bolster pillow and tie the ends with ribbon. If you want a tailored fit with no gaps, stitch Velcro to the fabric where the edges meet. Spell out a message with cord and finish it with a flourish of pompons.
WORKSHOP **PAGE 122**

WHAT'S YOUR PLEASURE?
THE COLLECTED GIFT!

Rather than a single item, serve up a series of gifts on a tray, all revolving around a theme. If you have a friend who adores the wonderful "Thin Man" movies of the 1930s and 40s, in which William Powell and Myrna Loy always seem to be stirring up martinis, present him with some Art Deco barware and the trimmings, including vintage cocktail napkins, promotional recipe booklets, and even special olives. For the aunt who cherishes her quiet cup of tea, a handmade cozy surrounded by cups and saucers, special leaf blends, a teaball, and a pretty teapot are perfectly charming.
WORKSHOP **PAGE 123**

Pipecleaner smoke and **gumdrop** windows…that's what **gingerbread houses** are made of.

THE LITTLEST VILLAGE

Gingerbread castles are traditional centerpieces at Christmas, but we prefer a village: it's not quite so grand and it's definitely more charming. As huge as a project like a village might seem, oddly enough, completing it won't add to the frenzy of the holiday if you make it a family event. There's something soothing about rolling out the dough, cutting it, and decorating it. What can you use as trimmings? While the dough is resting—it needs twenty-four hours before you can handle it—check out the glorious world of "building materials" beyond royal icing.

When you decorate the village, it's not entirely different from creating a real house. Construct the major architectural features like doorways and windows first. For rooftops and chimneys, you can relax the outlines a bit. Since you're creating the look of snow, icing can appear to be melting and drifting, so children needn't worry about coloring within the lines,

❄ **WORKSHOP PAGES** 123-124

COME STAY A WHILE
IN GINGERBREAD TOWN

Rather like the set of an old movie Western, the buildings of our gingerbread town are actually one-dimensional. They are glued to the backs of picture-frame easels for support. Call out the building materials: twin candy canes are "pillars" on either side of the village. Lollipops inserted in gum drop bases become stop signs on the village streets. To fill out the snow scene, add white cotton batting or shredded coconut. Above, an icicle overhang cut from a long sheet of paper enhances this chilly scene of winter. Any tabletop tree—be it bottlebrush or a candle—can sit in the town square. Traditionally, gingerbread towns rest on tables, but this one is elevated to an open cupboard, where every nook is a decorating opportunity. We stocked the lower alcoves with decorations and treats, but you could add on to the gingerbread town instead, perhaps with farmhouses and barns on the outskirts of the village, surrounded by white picket fences.

THE NIGHT BEFORE CHRISTMAS

Greet Santa
with decorations
here, there,
everywhere!

ure as Santa loves cookies, as Rudolph's nose is holly-berry red, as Aunt Frieda will knit you an extra-long scarf, the climax of the season will always be Christmas morning. But truth be told, it's the anticipation that shapes the memories adults and children alike will come to treasure. An afternoon baking cookies, a weekend whipping up displays for the yard, an evening caroling in the crisp winter air...these are the stuff of sugarplum dreams.

Throughout the season, put a flourish in every day. In the evenings, make a ritual of reading a Christmas story by the glow of the tree lights. Gather around the

piano to sing Christmas carols. Of course, one of our

most enjoyable ways to spend time

together is decorating. These

Christmas projects can be family

affairs; adults tackle the more

challenging crafts and little ones

work on their own level, stringing

ribbons through buttons, cutting

paper snowflakes with craft

scissors, constructing paper chains. These times

offer the best Christmas gift, a memory that will be

treasured. Tuck away those snowflakes and paper

chains; you'll cherish them someday.

BREIT LIGHTS

Previous page: Imagine a chilly winter night, the kind that frosts windows and trims the garden with icicles. Guests hurry from their cars, eager to shed their heavy coats and bask in the warmth of your hearth. To speed their footsteps and lead the way, set a pair of beacons on your doorstep. More durable than luminaries, frosted candles take just minutes to make. ❄ WORKSHOP PAGE 124

WELCOME WINTER

If you have a sheltered terrace, turn it into a holiday tableau. Galvanized buckets wear icicle garlands, while a wreath sports holly leaves that have been cut from the pages of old Christmas songbooks. And what's that tucked among the greenery? Tiny resin caroler figurines are secured in place by wire. You can create a similar effect with those little folks meant to populate model train villages.

JINGLING ALL THE WAY

Since one-horse open sleighs aren't quite so common anymore, we have to find new ways to bring a pleasant jingle to the holiday season. Try putting together tinkling ornaments—they're easy and quick to make, and they're environmentally correct because they recycle old Christmas cards. To make one, cut an image from a holiday card; we chose a bell with a cameo portrait of skaters from a card that we found in a box at the flea market. Attach crafts store bells (any color will work) to the bottom so that they dangle and catch every breeze. Hole punch an opening in the top, thread wide ribbon through the card and tie a multi-loop bow. Hang the ornament from a wreath on the front door.

Dear Friend

It's fun to rethink everyday objects for the holidays—fill teapots with fresh holly, arrange vintage toys on the mantel, and wrap a quilt around the base of the tree. Set up a display of your white art pottery along a windowsill and pile the pieces with red glass balls.

Yours,
Mary

BESAME MUCHO

'Tis the season for displays of affection, so bring on the kissing balls! Hang one by the front door, another by the back door. Hang one in the hall and one in the kitchen. Make these sweet reminders to embrace each other part of everyday during the holidays. Kissing balls involve no more than a Styrofoam ball, a glue gun, and flower petals or evergreens like juniper, white pine, and spruce. They can be made with pinecones or fresh roses; they might be sprigs of winterberry and they can even be covered with chocolate kisses. Who could have too many kisses?

IT'S A PARTY!

CAROL·FEST

A Little Night Music

We'll Play: Everyone gets a family songbook and after a singing stroll, returns to a room dressed in lush garlands, twinkly lights, and kissing balls.

We'll Feast: To soothe hardworking vocal cords, indulge in homemade potato chips, a chicken stew, and jolly chocolate snowman cake.

Singing can be the most joyous expression of the holidays. Do you remember the scene in "It's a Wonderful Life" when George Bailey is reunited with his family and friends, and, as his daughter plays along on the piano, they all sing "Hark! The Herald Angels Sing?" Consider hosting a party just to sing Christmas carols. You'll really be surprised by how enthusiastically everyone joins in after a bit of warming up. Not only are you all together in song, but everyone gets the benefit of some music therapy too.

SING, CHOIRS OF ANGELS

Choir boy and girl candles have been popular holiday decorations for years. You'll often find cardboard labels on their bases stating they were made by the Gurley Candle Company in Buffalo, New York. Gather your own choir and place them on unusual perches: in birdcages, under glass domes, or in front of a mirror.

THE OFFICIAL FAMILY SONGBOOK

Help guests remember the lyrics of their favorite carols and give them a party keepsake at the same time with individual songbooks. Photocopy pages of beloved old tunes (back to back works best) and laminate them with clear plastic; this serves to preserve and weatherproof them in case you go caroling in a snow flurry. If you're really ambitious, you can compose original, personalized lyrics to carols that everyone can sing out.

The best carols for a crowd include "We Wish You a Merry Christmas," "Joy to the World," "Frosty the Snowman," "Deck the Halls," and, naturally, "Here Comes Santa Claus." Have extra songbooks on hand for carolers to take as favors.

A caroling party can come in many guises. You may be lucky enough to have a piano, but you can also sing to recorded instrumentals or take a brisk hike around the neighborhood singing a capella. One of the best ideas: put your show on the road and visit a local hospital or nursing home, or make a stop at the fire department. Audiences will be absolutely enchanted.

Pamper hardworking vocal guests with a warming supper of chicken stew and soothe their tired throats with a sparkling cranberry punch. End the evening with hefty slices of rich chocolate snowman cake. This is a cozy little party, nothing fancy or fussy, ideal anytime during the holidays. Relax and don't worry if you're singing off-key.

B-r-r-r-r!
Baby, it's cold outside.

JOIN THE PARTY
Inspire revelers to sing the night away. Hang garlands strung with white fairy lights everywhere—around doors and windows, on banisters, frames, and bookshelves. Wrap pot plants with Mylar; tie on some jingle bells with silver organdy bows. Create a casual buffet where guests can gravitate: Cranberry-Ginger Punch with its festive jewel-toned color and bobbing lemon slices is so pretty. When your dessert is the extraordinary Snowman Cake, it deserves to be on a pedestal. Then light the candles and enjoy one pitch-perfect evening.

PANTRY PAGES 100-102

MAY I HAVE MORE, PLEASE?
Reward carolers for their bold efforts dashing through the snow with a heartwarming meal. A chicken stew fortified with bacon and Burgundy has a stick-to-your-ribs goodness. Served alongside are crispy homemade baked potato chips, destined to become one of your signature dishes. They're so delicious that however many you think you need, there still won't be enough. Kids can enjoy the chips plain, though adults will appreciate a selection of pesto dips. PANTRY PAGE 99

The CHRISTMAS PAGEANT

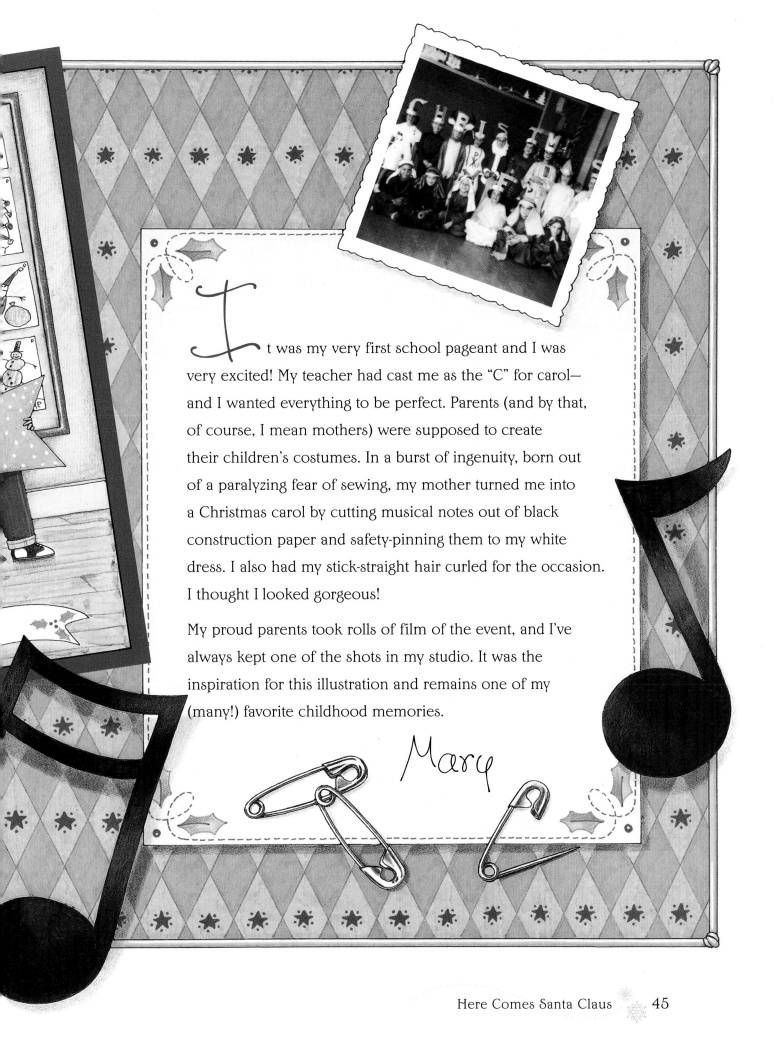

It was my very first school pageant and I was very excited! My teacher had cast me as the "C" for carol—and I wanted everything to be perfect. Parents (and by that, of course, I mean mothers) were supposed to create their children's costumes. In a burst of ingenuity, born out of a paralyzing fear of sewing, my mother turned me into a Christmas carol by cutting musical notes out of black construction paper and safety-pinning them to my white dress. I also had my stick-straight hair curled for the occasion. I thought I looked gorgeous!

My proud parents took rolls of film of the event, and I've always kept one of the shots in my studio. It was the inspiration for this illustration and remains one of my (many!) favorite childhood memories.

Mary

DECK THE WALLS

After the Christmas tree, a lushly decorated hearth is probably the second most important area in the holiday home. Creating one is a matter of building the layers, perhaps a little each day. The mantel is treated to two helpings of greenery: one on the top, with a black-and-white check ribbon winding through to harmonize the elements, and another beneath, hung garland-style from teacup hooks, with its own red-and-white check ribbon bows. A plain evergreen wreath from the nursery can be customized in minutes by wiring on small toys and ornaments. Decorated with sewing scraps and craft box odds and ends, the stockings follow in the tradition of the American quilt. (If you don't have a mantel, your stockings can still be hung with care and charm. Dangle them on the rungs of a ladderback chair, from a bookcase, or even from a coat rack.) Tuck in two or three Christmas mice and some snowmen; there really isn't a reason why Santa shouldn't give his reindeer a rest and come with a handsome Airedale. The tree-shaped gingham and rickrack cardholder at the center of the mantel provides a vertical complement to the framed mirror alongside; slipping in the day's cards adds new interest. ❄ WORKSHOP

PAGES 125-126

OUT OF THE BOX

Looking like giant candles, mailing tubes from the stationery store deliver gifts in a more intriguing fashion. Just what gifts could go in tubes? Think socks, scarves, mittens, pajamas, paint pens, posters—almost anything you'd put in a box. Cinch the wrapping paper 'round the ends and twist à la Tootsie Roll style. Finish with the flourish of a bow and a tag!

TAG: YOU'RE IT!

Even an ordinary-looking gift becomes special with a handmade gift tag. These are collaged from paper and stickers. Chunky retro Bakelite buttons attached with glue provide a touch of glamour (stack 'em up for a multicolor effect). Thread ribbon through the holes to anchor them to the ribbons already on the packages. Pretty beads and even vintage belt buckles work too. We wrote greetings on the tags with a metallic paint pen, but fountain pens also create a distinctive look.

Bow Monde

Ribbons aren't just for wrapping gifts—especially at Christmas! Little girls look sweet with beautiful ribbons tied round their heads into floppy bows; so do their moms. In the home, trail sparkly organdy ribbon among clear glass ornaments on a tabletop. Accent greenery with tartan patterns. Weave ribbons through the arms of chandeliers. Suspend ornaments from streamers or rickrack on windows and mantels. Drape dining chairs with strands of silk sashing. Spray-paint twigs white or gold and cinch them with grosgrain to set up before the hearth.

TAKE a BOUGH

A Gathering to Trim the Tree

We'll Play: Everyone pitches in
getting decorations, whispy garlands, and glittering
ornaments on the Christmas tree.

We'll Feast: Hard work deserves sumptuous food:
steak pinwheels, rice and peas, and a divine chocolate
and amaretto cheesecake.

The tree has been chosen and brought home. There it is, in its stand, a fragrant tower of green awaiting its holiday destiny. Since it's the most beautiful, perfect Christmas tree ever (do we say that every year?), it surely deserves the most spectacular ornaments you can imagine.

Bring out all the sentimental favorites, each one sparking a story or a memory. It's fun to introduce new ones to the mix too—and they don't have to come from the store. There are all sorts of possibilities beyond traditional ornaments. With hooks and wires, you can hang most anything, including stuffed animals and little toys. Drape costume jewelry among the boughs; roll leftover quilt batting into snowballs. Cotton batting, by the way, makes a fluffy, snowy tree

skirt. Think dolls: vintage dresses hang on the tree with clothespins, paper-doll garlands clasp hands in a dance around the branches. Mary herself once turned a favorite old doll into a tree-topping angel, with paper doilies as the wings and mother of pearl buttons for the halo.

Of course, when you assemble a large group of trimmers to help with the tree, you must have a plan of action or your fabulous fir could end up

ORGANIZE YOUR ELVES
WITH ORNAMENT BOXES

Not only do these bandboxes make handy holders during your tree-trimming party, they also offer safe, permanent residence to the ornaments within. Ordinary hatboxes dressed up with gift wrap or vintage wallpaper are all you need. A simple color scheme works best.

From the forest to you—
a tree of dreams

decorated on one side and not the other! Lights go on first. Layer several strands of small fairy lights with chunkier bulbs. Work from the base of the trunk up unless you're adding a garland. Beaded garlands tend to look best hanging in swags from branch to branch.

Vary the sizes of ornaments. Position the lighter ones on the outer tips of the branches and those that are heavier closer in to the trunk, as if they had sprouted there as naturally as pine-cones. Go ahead and hang your child's preschool creations front and center. Smaller drawings can be framed and hung every year, along with your most precious glass ornaments.

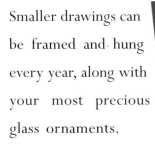

BRANCHING OUT

Sometimes it's easy to get carried away and pile on so many ornaments that you can't see the poor tree underneath. An airy garland of chenille yarn twisted into spirally loops, with tatted snowflakes and pompon snowballs sewn on at irregular intervals for a natural effect, gives the tree some breathing space. Though the ornaments have handmade touches, many are simply pre-existing designs that were customized for the tree. The tin snowflakes, for instance, are embellished with clip-art Santa faces glued to their centers. The tree-topper is simply a larger version of the same thing. We painted and glittered papier-mâché stars. Since the tree has a neutral foundation of white and gold, jewel-tone red lights contrast against the serene backdrop.

GIFTS TO WISH ON

This irresistibly naughty little scottie is a favorite of Mary's. It's available where her products are sold and it's a perfect gift for visiting children. The nifty Christmas tree boxes not only serve as decorations, their lids open to reveal surprises inside. Découpage papier-mâché boxes with photocopies of childhood Christmas pictures or kids' holiday artwork, or with images from clip-art books, peel-away polka dots, and wooden letters… whatever comes to mind. Tuck in a simple little present; attach a ribbon to the box and hang it from the tree. ❄ WORKSHOP **PAGE 126**

Christmas with Mary Engelbreit

HO-HO HOSTING

While guests are busy dressing up those evergreen branches, you'll be setting a table that so overflows with Christmas cheer, even the chairs are decorated. Vintage holiday table-cloths and bolts of Christmas fabric create the placemats. In fact, these are reversible, so they can appear at a tree-trimming party and again at Christmas dinner. Vegetables are first to arrive at the table, followed by a platter of steak pinwheels. WORKSHOP **PAGE** 127, PANTRY **PAGE** 103

THE MOUSE TAKES
THE CHEESE...CAKE

You might have heard about the fellow in Clement Clarke Moore's poem, "A Visit From St. Nicholas," or maybe you remember the Mouse King from "The Nutcracker." In his latest incarnation, the Christmas Mouse has been transformed into a soigné felt ornament. He's given to lounging about in his dapper, comfy bathrobe and inviting himself to holiday parties, just like "The Mouse Who Came to Dinner." But will mice enjoy eating cheesecake? For grown-up people only, a double-decker creation with a layer of chocolate and another of amaretto-flavored cheesecake is downright heavenly. Served with hot coffee or tea, it's a lovely dessert to end an evening with friends. WORKSHOP **PAGES** 126, PANTRY **PAGE** 104

THE MORE THE MERRIER

At last, the long wait is over. Christmas is finally here! Draw friends and family near.

Whether it's one lunch for a handful of friends or a dozen parties of all sizes, some people seem to pull off holiday entertaining with total nonchalance. Just what makes it so easy for them?

These are hostesses who know the secrets of entertaining with joy. The fun comes in thinking about exciting ways to entertain that don't break the piggy bank but seem special and extravagant nonetheless.

What are these secrets? Here's one: Bake sweets often during the days of Christmas. The familiar, fragrant scent of holiday spices immediately transforms a room.

Another tip: Delegate to family members. For instance, your son could serve as a waiter while your daughter arranges cookie platters and candy dishes. Choose recipes based on simplicity as well as good taste.

Great parties aren't only about food, however. To add to the festivities, scatter simple board games around to keep guests busy. Dress pets for the holidays with ribbons on their collars. For children, have inexpensive gifts ready. A little present helps a youngster feel more comfortable in someone else's home. After all, comfort—and joy—are what it's all about.

CARD TRICKS

Previous page: Every corner is a decorating opportunity. Vintage playing cards tacked to a pantry with double-stick tape become holiday shelf liners. Bottlebrush trees and antique postcards fill the shelves with snowy scenes. Marquee letters spell out a greeting; you could easily substitute children's alphabet blocks.

PRETTY PLEASE, WITH SUGAR ON TOP

Even the glasses are kissed by holiday cheer. We dipped the rims in lemon juice, then twirled them in colored sugar to make festive goblets for a serving of holiday sorbet. You could also decorate wine glasses by tying ribbons around the stems—different colors help guests remember which is theirs.

OH, THE WEATHER OUTSIDE IS FRIGHTFUL

Why is the screen porch a holiday decorating Frontierland? How many houses have you seen with wonderful decorations that stop short at the front door, and resume safely inside? The good news is that the porch, whether it's in front or at the side of the house, is great fun to pull into the holiday swing. Dressed for the season, it offers welcome and shelter to everyone coming in, a place where they can let out their breath, peel off heavy boots, and begin to warm up. The porch can carry off less serious, more whimsical decorating treatments. We've given ours a tree of its own, complete with sparkly white lights. We've added holiday cheer to the furnishings by wrapping loose cushions in Christmas fabrics, laying a snowy cloth on the side table, and lighting candles throughout. A babies-breath wreath and decorations of evergreen and pinecones are abundant and harmonious companions to the textural stone walls. Now it's perfect for a party. How lucky we are to have a stack of cableknit throws that will keep us warm!

Rudolph and His Friends

You see them prancing across front lawns everywhere: reindeer made of logs, sticks, wire, and even bright white lights. Indoors, vintage reindeer are likely to be papier-mâché, celluloid, silver, ivorine, or, like teddy bears, stuffed fabric with furry coats. With their silent, gentle charm, families of reindeer fit right into any decorating plan. Whether they're inside or out, we like to move them around from day to day to surprise family and guests. After all, deer do get restless and enjoy a little roam about the area.

IT'S A PARTY!

Snow Picnic

A Nippy Porch Lunch

We'll Play: Fill the porch with Christmas decorations, hang snowflakes from the ceiling, invite the Snow Family, and set a picnic table.

We'll Feast: Stay warm with hearty turkey pot pies, some chocolate and marshmallow s'mores, and creamy hot peppermint chocolate.

Even if your calendar is positively packed from now until January 1st, you still want to spend time with family. Take the reins and create casual festivities to incorporate into everyday events. For instance, how about a picnic on the porch? Sure, it's a little nippy out there, but bring out a space heater or stoke up the wood stove and you'll be toasty in no time.

Ideally, you wake to a snow fantasy outside. Pull on the galoshes and spend the morning building not just a lone snowman but an entire family, complete with every imaginable accessory from apron to straw hat. Lunch then is a good opportunity to regroup for the afternoon and spend time together.

Plan a menu that's easy to carry out yet a little bit special. Remember, everyone will be ravenous, so make the fare substantial. Hearty, warming foods will neutralize the chill. Be sure to provide extra servings; after all, it's quite a feat to create a Snow Family.

PARTY HATS REQUIRED

Snowfolk are some of the jolliest souls around at Christmas. But you needn't wait for fresh fallen snow to invite them and their families to your celebrations. They're equally at home on mantels and holiday tables. Customize a set to mimic your family; a visit to the doll shop will yield tiny eyeglasses, necklaces and earrings, scarves and mufflers, and ribbons. Choose from blue, brown, and black buttons for the eyes. ❋ WORKSHOP **PAGE 128**

This unique party is an opportunity to bring some fabulous decorations to a room that's often ignored during the holiday. Keep your linen tablecloth in its drawer and create a country look on the table by tossing a plaid lap blanket or a patterned shawl over an undercloth of solid-colored fabric. An old quilt would also do the trick. On the table, pick some less familiar holiday colors: pewter with pearly white iron-stone or brown-and-

white transferware. We decorated our lunch table with bottlebrush trees, reindeer, and snowmen, but a birdhouse collection, jazzed up with tiny birds and miniwreaths, would be great too. Drape pine garlands about the porch: with its cool temperatures, all the evergreens you put out will last for weeks. For the same reason, the porch is a natural setting for a forest of small potted Alberta spruces; at winter's end, they can even be planted outdoors.

Let it snow, let it snow, please Let It Snow!

A TURKEY IN EVERY POT PIE AND A GIFT IN EVERY BOX

Turkey pot pie is especially appropriate for the holidays since it comes "giftwrapped" in its own pastry. Underneath, a surprise: fresh vegetables and subtle spices, instead of the usual soupy mix that characterizes so many frozen pot pies. PANTRY PAGE 105

Surprise family and guests with presents along the way. For a quilt-inspired look, boxes from the crafts store are découpaged with photocopies of fabric swatches. They make great carriers for candies and other treats nestled in paper cups. One sweet suggestion: try chocolate-dipped candied orange peel, a perfect light dessert after a hearty meal. WORKSHOP PAGE 129

FEASTING IN A WINTER WONDERLAND

The effect is magical, but the porch truly took minutes to decorate. Crafts-store snowflakes suspended from yarn twinkle in the sun. The picnic table is simply dressed with placemats and little trees. Golden pot pies in blue-and-white graniteware impart a lighthearted mood. Pull up a camp stool and dig in.

...AND NOW FOR
THE ENVELOPE, PLEASE

Gifts in envelopes are absolutely intriguing. Lots of envelopes hold cool cash, which is always in fine taste. But perhaps your envelope holds tickets to a sporting event or concert. If you're more sentimental, it might contain copies of nostalgic photos from other happy times—a snapshot of you and Cousin Tillie tobogganing down the slopes or trimming a long-ago tree. Ours are made from vellum and paper doilies, accentuated with buttons. Other easy choices are manila envelopes with a collage of antique papers, rubber stamps, and notions. But wait—there's more! Decorate card boxes with photocopies of Christmas images or family photographs; inscribe the year on each box and it becomes a handsome container for correspondence and keepsakes.

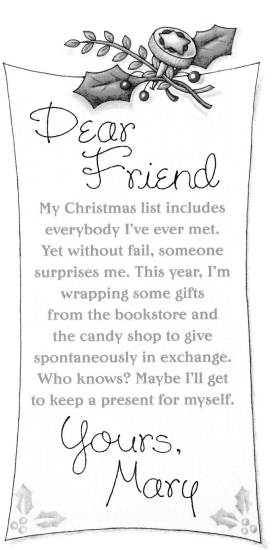

Dear Friend

My Christmas list includes everybody I've ever met. Yet without fail, someone surprises me. This year, I'm wrapping some gifts from the bookstore and the candy shop to give spontaneously in exchange. Who knows? Maybe I'll get to keep a present for myself.

Yours,
Mary

Christmas is a reason **to cut and paste again,** just like you did in **kindergarten.**

HAPPY TRAILS TO YOU

Here's a splendid example of the homemade gift at its best: a custom travel bag to carry jewelry, make-up, extra keys, and toiletries. It's thoughtful, inexpensive, quickly made, appropriate for just about everybody, and it's fun. Choose from sturdy retro fabrics and combine patterns and colors as you wish. Sometimes the print will even give a hint as to what's inside. If you want to make something especially for Christmas guests, search out lively holiday tablecloths from the 1950's and 60's. No wrapping required! ❄ WORKSHOP

PAGE 130

THE FAVOR OF YOUR COMPANY

A sweet parting indeed awaits guests. Echoing the shape of a Christmas tree, a stack of little treats is all ready to be taken home by guests at the end of the party. The sachets are pretty vintage handkerchiefs plump with wintery pot-pourri, tied with a length of saucy ribbon, and nestled on the three-tiered pedestal. You could also fill the sachets with trinkets—small bottles of fancy lotions and colognes, pastel hand soaps, bracelet charms, tiny gift books, refrigerator magnets, some choice marbles, jawbreakers—literally something for every guest to enjoy. If you've got a lot of men and boys in your life, you'll probably want to replace some of the hankies with bandanas.

UNDER·WRAPS

A Treasure Hunt

We'll Play: Each guest gets a number,
then sets off to find her own special hidden gift.

We'll Feast: The menu is hidden food:
pork enchiladas, baby apple pies baked in paper bags,
and beggars' purses with sweet and savory fillings.

Hunting is synonymous with the holidays. First we must find perfect gifts…for twenty-five people. We must find the wrapping paper, the scotch tape, the gift cards, and then we must find all the presents we have stashed away in such good hiding places that we no longer remember where they are.

Still, who doesn't love a good mystery—and that's what a hidden gifts party is all about. Make the invitations intriguing; they could be cut into pieces à la jigsaw puzzle, or cut in the shape of a question mark, or folded into

PUT YOUR THINKING CAPS ON

Hang impossible-to-miss hints to your hiding places on a bottlebrush tree. Each guest receives a number which represents a package, and the note attached gives some clue to the location. Make the clues difficult enough to be interesting, but not so cryptic that guests end up walking around in circles.

HE CAME TO LIFE ONE DAY

A pretty snowman bottle becomes a container for a specially-flavored vodka; Frosty's top hat is actually the bottle stopper. For a gift to delight just about any grown-up, infuse vodka with berries or cherries or cranberries two weeks before Christmas. Homemade flavored vodka has a wonderful fresh flavor hard to find in commercial products. The drawstring sack is reusable and easy to sew. PANTRY **PAGE 107**, WORKSHOP **PAGE 131**

What's peeking out from under that beggar's purse? Could it be a clue?

origami shapes. Whatever you choose, just make them fun to set the tone.

The object of the party is for guests to find gifts that you've stashed away around the house. Start them off with clues that lead onward to yet another clue written fortune-cookie style, and eventually to the gift itself. Think outdoors. Imagine finding a good bottle of Champagne that's nestled in the crook of a tree!

Give children their own set of clues to age-appropriate gifts. When you tuck gifts within gifts, the effect is as captivating as your first Russian nesting doll.

You needn't spend a fortune on gifts. The challenge is concealing them. Think of hiding presents in pouches of velvet and other opulent materials. For the children, stock up on chocolate coins, unusual beads, stickers, Pez dispensers, miniature cars, balls and jacks.

Here's your opportunity to present guests with the gift they'll appreciate most: a relaxing time, enjoying the pleasure of good company.

THAT'S THE TICKET

A night at the opera? A matinée with the Rockettes? The gift-giving ticket possibilities are endless: front row seats at a dog show, a tennis event, the latest Broadway play. Present coupons to babysit the little ones, walk the dog, pick up dry-cleaning.

TIERS OF JOY

You can double, triple, even quadruple the area of your serving station with tiered trays. Pile footed cake stands on each other or enlist a garden plant stand. Offer appetizers that can be enjoyed with only the aid of a napkin. The most appropriate menu for a hidden gifts party is, of course, hidden food. Everything is tucked within its own wrapping. Beggars purses with a variety of savory and sweet fillings remain a surprise until they're bitten into. Even the tiny apple pies were baked hidden inside paper bags! PANTRY 109-110

OPEN YOUR HEART ~
OPEN IT WIDE:
SOMEONE IS STANDING OUTSIDE

very year, I try to do at least one illustration that focuses on the religious significance of Christmas. While these are not always the most commercially successful, it's important to me to recognize in some way (and my way, of course, is on paper), the true meaning of the holiday. My inspiration for this drawing was the quote. I just love it. I always have since the first time I read it—although I don't know where it came from or to whom it is attributed.

So often it seems that Santa is the main focus at Christmas time, but in this illustration he's trying to show you that there is Somebody more important waiting for you to open your heart. This has become one of my favorite Christmas cards, and it's been popular in the shops.

Mary

Christmas with Mary Engelbreit

OPEN FOR THE HOLIDAYS

Guests will be charmed by this frieze of houses decorated with rickrack and ribbon. With cut-out doors and shutters that swing open and shut, the houses are symbols of your open-door policy. Attach them to a banister with a garland of greenery and flourishes of candy canes and faux fruit, or let them decorate a sheltered door, illuminated by twinkling white lights so that the display is still visible after dark. In fact, the house theme could also be three-dimensional: recycle oatmeal boxes, potato chip cans, and other sturdy containers. Build an entire village, which would look as welcoming under the tree as it would on the front porch. You could even bring a pineapple, that timeless symbol of hospitality, to your holiday tabletop. ❄ WORKSHOP PAGE 132

Dear Friend

I like my Christmas everywhere. Yes, I decorate the powder room. I hang a wreath in the laundry room. I put little trees on dressers, little Santas on closet shelves, and little reindeer on the mailbox. Why not? It's about so much more than the tree in the living room!

Yours, Mary

IT'S CHRISTMAS— THE WHOLE HOUSE IS CLEAN!

Casual holiday entertaining encourages guests to drift from room to room. Share your home with visitors by dressing each area with some sort of decoration. A guest bedroom is readied for its company: holiday postcards are poised on a tea tray that is actually a small stool. Slips of gingham-printed chiffon ribbon are tied in soft bows for the dresser, curtain tie-backs, and to decorate the bed post. The dresser mirror is perked up with a colorful foil and copper wire garland that takes minutes to make and lasts forever. Just before guests arrive, light a festive votive candle for an instant touch that makes a big, welcoming difference. ❄ WORK- SHOP **PAGE 133**

BE WARM INSIDE & OUT

IT'S A PARTY!

OPEN HOUSE

Christmas Is Finally Here

We'll Play: All the holiday best is out and ready.

We'll Feast: Eat all day—glazed ham, fresh biscuits, the world's best sweet potato dish, and eggnog. Eat again at night—ham biscuits, sweet potato pancakes, and eggnog shakes.

The Danish word "Hygge" means that when you open your house, you open your heart. Hygge conjures a sense of coziness and warmth. A house can have hygge; so can a meal, a story, a get-together, a person. When the Danes throw parties, they're never stuffy affairs, but rather joyous events that tend to last for hours, from day to night. What an elegant model for a Christmas open house. We've created one for you that can be orchestrated way in advance and pulled off pretty effortlessly, from brunch to supper.

The key to a day of successful entertaining is preparation. Select versatile foods that can be made ahead and reinvented through the day—

like a great ham, tasty biscuits, a sweet potato dish. Flourishes help guests feel appreciated. Serve coffee in an antique pot. Give everyone a memento of the day—perhaps a home-baked specialty or a half bottle of dessert wine.

DOLLOPS OF DOILIES

Get out your doilies and dress up the dining room chairs with holiday slipcovers. Drape a tea towel over each chairback and top it with an old-fashioned crocheted doily. Layer more tea towels on the buffet table; replace them as they become soiled. Present a steady parade of dishes (overleaf), and tell guests what each dish is with a colorful flag. By unanimous decree you will be proclaimed Queen of Christmas!

PANTRY **PAGES** 111–112

Cultivate a feeling of welcome by scattering decorations through every room in the house. But don't be a perfectionist—this is not about erecting a centerpiece worthy of a flower show. Instead, you will be creating a series of lively— silly, even—tableaux for guests to enjoy. Be spontaneous: Fill up those teacups, trophies, and compotes with vintage ornaments or figural lightbulbs in Santa shapes. Hang tissue-paper snowflakes in windows (let the kids make them!). Dangle little paper partridges from a feather tree. A construction-paper-chain garland would be charming and disarming over the powder room mirror. If your holiday buffet is an annual event, gather photos from past parties and let them inspire you. They can be framed and hung on the tree, across the mantel, or in the entry hall. Scan them and print them as place cards. Now that's personal.

Today is not for dieting; it's for fulfilling food fantasies.

ALL THAT GLITTERS

Glass is the ideal way to bridge day-into-night entertaining. During the afternoon, glass sparkles as sunlight catches its facets, while by night glass gleams in candle glow. Best of all, whatever its provenance, all glassware seems to go together, whether it's vintage and new, whether it's rare crystal or jelly glass. Mix up classic patterns and unexpected uses: For instance, a hobnail pickle dish could serve dips, while a bubble glass dessert bowl might hold olives. Perhaps a stemmed sherbet cup serves a portion of sweet potato casserole; a beaded relish plate presents spiced nuts at cocktails or chocolates after dinner.

IN A CHRISTMAS BONNET?

More so than with any other form of entertaining, presentation is key when you serve food buffet style. For this reason, choose dishes that have a bit of sparkle or a touch of whimsy. In this case, we tweaked the presentation of traditional panna cotta slightly, drizzling the strawberry sauce and arranging the garnishes in such a way that the custards resemble small hats, complete with mint feathers. PANTRY PAGE 113

Oh by gosh, by golly, Here Comes Santa Claus!

Think of it as Act Two. The first group of revelers—folks with young children and guests who have other dinner plans—have moved on. Now the party takes on a glittering nighttime mood. In fact, evening affords you decorating opportunities more varied and imaginative than you might consider for day. Just a few strings of tiny white fairylights create a romantic look. Nestle them amid evergreens to enliven dark spots like, for instance, those awkward spaces over cabinets. Let windowboxes bloom with pine boughs festooned with twinkling pinlights. Drape icicle lights over an arbor so that guests can enjoy the view out-doors. A small bench will host a romantic couple in an impromptu snowfall. Inside, decorate potted plants like palms and Norfolk pine in the same way, but add glass chandelier prisms for up-close glamour. As dusk falls, all you need do is flick a switch and let the gaiety begin.

YOU CAN BRING IT WITH YOU

"Which is my drink?" is such a common refrain at parties. Solve this problem instantly with individual glass cups and trays to keep track of beverages. Customize trays for the holiday with painted designs or découpaged images. To make it easy for guests to nibble as they flow from room to room, serve plenty of finger foods, such as these individual plum cakes. ❋ PANTRY PAGE 115

MOVABLE FEASTING

Encourage guests to set up their own dining stations wherever they please. Any nook will do, even a corner card table fitted with a holiday cloth. Look around your rooms and consider the possibilities. For example, you might line up champagne glasses on the mantel, interspersed with rosemary topiaries. Or a sidetable between armchairs could be the ideal place for a pair of guests to take dessert while having a tête à tête. For evening diners, a feast of ham biscuits, cranberry sauce, and creamy eggnog shakes will satisfy the hungriest while still tempting the fullest. ❋ PANTRY PAGES 114, 115

LET'S DO THIS AGAIN NEXT YEAR

Now that the party's over, don't rush to clean up just yet. Take a moment to relax in the waning glow of the candlelight and page through the comments in the guest book. There is Uncle Jake's inimitable handwriting with his traditional Christmas poem. And a sweet drawing of Henry the dog by your young niece. So many memories were made today. Perhaps you have a few thoughts to jot down as well, before they disappear into the whirlwind of the holiday season. In fact, it's a good idea to write with archival-quality ink so that the words never fade. Later, you could turn the guest book into a memory book by adding photographs. Tomorrow, when you do set about cleaning up, don't throw away all those old candle stubs. With craft store supplies, you can melt them to make new candles in pretty jars for your next gathering...which could be just days away!

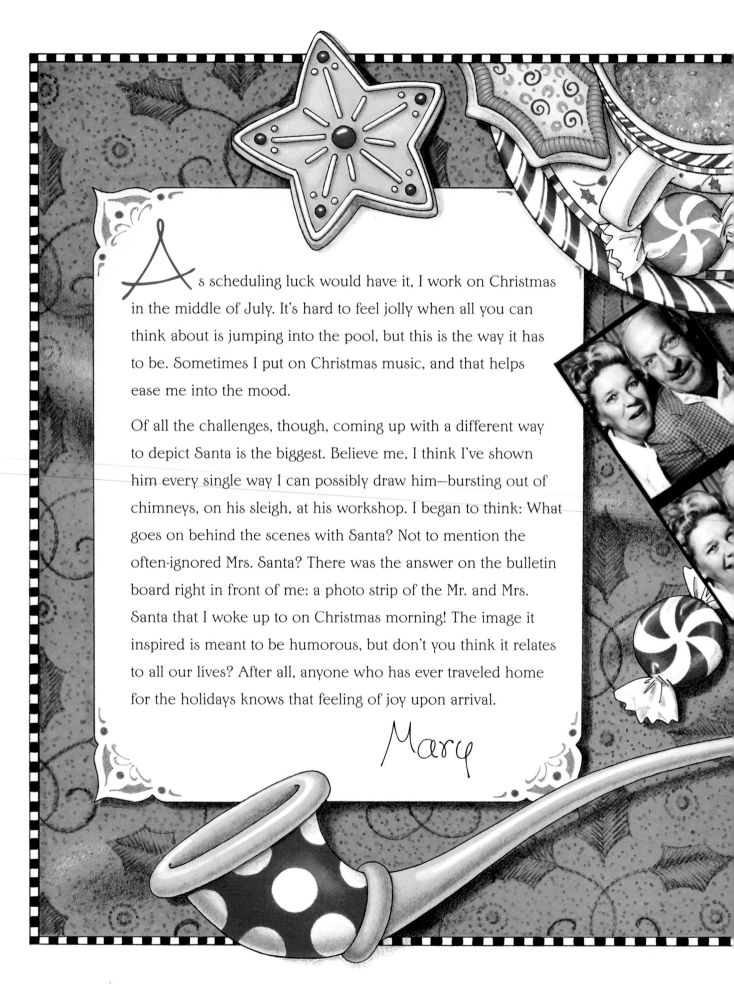

As scheduling luck would have it, I work on Christmas in the middle of July. It's hard to feel jolly when all you can think about is jumping into the pool, but this is the way it has to be. Sometimes I put on Christmas music, and that helps ease me into the mood.

Of all the challenges, though, coming up with a different way to depict Santa is the biggest. Believe me, I think I've shown him every single way I can possibly draw him—bursting out of chimneys, on his sleigh, at his workshop. I began to think: What goes on behind the scenes with Santa? Not to mention the often-ignored Mrs. Santa? There was the answer on the bulletin board right in front of me: a photo strip of the Mr. and Mrs. Santa that I woke up to on Christmas morning! The image it inspired is meant to be humorous, but don't you think it relates to all our lives? After all, anyone who has ever traveled home for the holidays knows that feeling of joy upon arrival.

Mary

PANTRY

Holidays transform good food into great food. Somehow, everything tastes extra-yummy when it's eaten in front of a glowing tree or from a mittened hand or before a crackling fireplace. You've already got a pretty terrific Christmas atmosphere working in your home, so when you plan party menus look for real crowd-pleasers. Start with your family favorites, and try some of ours. Yum!

Baked Brie with Praline-Mustard Glaze

Brie's rich, buttery flavor has a slight tang. Here it's underscored by the crunchy sweetness of praline-mustard glaze.

One 5-ounce piece ripe Brie
Half 8-ounce jar praline-mustard glaze
2 tablespoons chopped pecans, for garnish

1. Preheat the oven to 400°F.

2. If desired, trim the rind from the Brie. Cut the Brie into chunks and place in a small ovenproof serving dish. Bake for 5 minutes, or until the cheese is bubbly on top.

3. Pour the praline-mustard glaze over the Brie. Return to the oven to heat the glaze, about 2 to 3 minutes. Gently stir the glaze to mix just a bit, not completely. Sprinkle with the pecans.

4. Place the serving dish on a heatproof serving platter.

Serves 4 to 6

■ **SERVE IT WITH**

Melted Brie is rich on its own; combined with praline-mustard glaze, it's downright decadent. To control the richness, serve this pairing with assorted plain crackers like water biscuits. Granny Smith apples are wonderfully crunchy and tart companions with the cheese and crackers.

Spinach Soup

Few dishes offer greater return than homemade soup; in cold weather, there just isn't anything so satisfying.

3 tablespoons butter
3 tablespoons flour
8 cups chicken stock
2 pounds spinach, trimmed
  and finely chopped
1/8 teaspoon ground
  nutmeg
1 teaspoon salt
1/4 teaspoon freshly
  ground pepper
1 thin baguette, cut into 1/4-inch slices
1/2 cup freshly grated Parmesan cheese

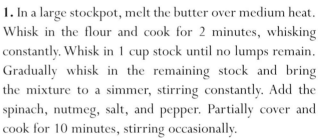

1. In a large stockpot, melt the butter over medium heat. Whisk in the flour and cook for 2 minutes, whisking constantly. Whisk in 1 cup stock until no lumps remain. Gradually whisk in the remaining stock and bring the mixture to a simmer, stirring constantly. Add the spinach, nutmeg, salt, and pepper. Partially cover and cook for 10 minutes, stirring occasionally.

2. Transfer the soup to a blender, in batches if necessary, and puree. Return to the pot and keep warm.

3. Meanwhile, preheat the broiler. Place the slices of baguette on baking sheets and sprinkle Parmesan over each slice. Broil for 3 to 4 minutes, or until the cheese is lightly browned. Immediately remove from the broiler.

4. Transfer the soup to a tureen or individual serving bowls and top with the toasts.

Serves 4 to 6

■ **VEGETARIAN SOUP**

Replace the chicken stock with vegetable stock and increase the salt and pepper to taste. The soup will be just as flavorful and delicious.

Santa's Pantry

For platters of good-looking holiday tea sandwiches, look in your cookie-cutter drawer. Make the sandwiches, then cut out the shapes of bells, Christmas trees, stars, reindeer, and Santa boots. Finish the look by spreading the edges of the sandwich with soft butter or mayonnaise and dipping them into chopped fresh herbs.

Smoked Salmon and Dill Sandwiches

Salmon and dill, a classic Scandinavian combo, is right at home for a winter gathering.

2 tablespoons minced fresh dill
6 tablespoons (¾ stick) butter, at room temperature
Pinch of salt
16 slices pumpernickel bread
8 ounces thinly sliced smoked salmon

1. In a small bowl, combine the dill with the butter and salt, mixing well.

2. Lay the bread on a work surface. Spread half the slices with a thin layer of dill-butter; top with a layer of salmon. Top with the remaining bread.

3. With a 2½-inch cookie cutter, cut out 2 shapes from each sandwich, or cut off the crusts and cut each sandwich into triangles. Arrange the sandwiches on a serving plate, cover with plastic wrap, and refrigerate.

4. About 20 minutes before serving, remove the sandwiches from the refrigerator and allow them to come to room temperature.

Serves 4 to 6

Cucumber and Goat Cheese Sandwiches

Zesty, creamy goat cheese is balanced by the fresh snap of cucumber in these modern English teatime sandwiches. The richness of the brioche is a fine complement. For more crunch, sprinkle chopped toasted walnuts over the goat cheese.

16 thin slices brioche
About 4 ounces soft goat cheese, at room temperature
1 large cucumber, peeled and thinly sliced

1. Lay the brioche slices on a work surface. Spread each with a thin layer of goat cheese. Arrange a thin layer of cucumbers on the remaining slices. Place the remaining brioche slices on the cucumber, goat cheese side down.

2. With a 2½-inch cookie cutter, cut out 2 shapes from each sandwich, or cut off the crusts and cut each sandwich into triangles. Arrange the sandwiches on a serving plate, cover with plastic wrap, and refrigerate.

3. About 20 minutes before serving, remove the sandwiches from the refrigerator and allow them to come to room temperature.

Serves 4 to 6

Peanut Butter and Jelly Sandwiches

Dressed in festive shapes for the holidays, this classic charms guests of all ages. If making ahead, cover with plastic wrap.

24 thin slices white bread
About $\frac{1}{2}$ cup creamy peanut butter
$\frac{1}{4}$ cup seedless raspberry jam

1. Lay the bread on a work surface. Spread half the slices with about $\frac{1}{2}$ tablespoon peanut butter each. Spread about 1 teaspoon raspberry jam on the peanut butter. Place the remaining slices on the jam.

2. With a $2\frac{1}{2}$-inch cookie cutter, cut 1 or 2 shapes from each sandwich, or cut off the crusts and cut each sandwich into triangles. Arrange the sandwiches on a serving plate and serve at room temperature.

Serves 4 to 6

Crunchy Peanut Brittle

Homemade candy is perfect at Christmas—actually, we think it's perfect any time!

$1\frac{1}{2}$ cups sugar
$\frac{2}{3}$ cup light corn syrup
$\frac{2}{3}$ cup plus $1\frac{1}{2}$ teaspoons water
1 teaspoon vanilla extract
$\frac{1}{2}$ teaspoon baking soda
$\frac{1}{2}$ teaspoon salt
2 tablespoons unsalted butter
$\frac{2}{3}$ cup unsalted peanuts, chopped

1. Generously butter a large baking sheet.

2. In a heavy saucepan, combine the sugar, corn syrup, and $\frac{2}{3}$ cup water. Stir constantly over medium heat until the mixture boils. Cover the pan and boil for 3 minutes. Uncover and boil until the mixture registers 250°F on a candy thermometer, about 5 minutes.

3. Meanwhile, in a small bowl, combine the remaining $1\frac{1}{2}$ teaspoons water and the vanilla, baking soda, and salt.

4. Add the butter and peanuts to the saucepan. Continue cooking until the mixture turns a light golden color, 3 to 5 minutes. Immediately remove the pan from the heat.

5. Add the baking soda mixture to the peanut mixture and stir until the mixture is thoroughly combined.

6. Pour the brittle onto the prepared baking sheet and allow to cool completely. Break the brittle into small pieces. Store in an airtight container for up to 3 days.

Serves 8

Anise-Scented Sugar Cookies

With cookie in hand, you're still a kid. These festive, licorice-scented creations will have you raiding the kitchen at midnight.

¾ cup granulated sugar

10 tablespoons
(1¼ sticks)
butter, at room
temperature

2 tablespoons milk

2 teaspoons vanilla
extract

¾ teaspoon anise
extract

1 large egg

2 cups flour

1 teaspoon baking powder

½ teaspoon salt

1½ cups confectioners' sugar, sifted

About ¼ cup water

Assorted food colors

Silver dragées, for decorating

1. In the large bowl of an electric mixer, beat the granulated sugar and butter at low speed until blended. Increase the speed to high and beat until the mixture is light and creamy. Reduce the speed to low and add the milk, vanilla, anise, and egg. Beat until blended.

2. In a medium bowl, mix the flour, baking powder, and salt. With the mixer on low speed, beat the flour mixture into the butter mixture until just blended.

3. Divide the dough in half and shape into 2 balls; flatten the balls slightly. Wrap each ball in plastic wrap and refrigerate for at least 1 hour.

4. Preheat the oven to 350°F.

5. On a lightly floured surface with a floured rolling pin, roll 1 ball of dough to an ⅛-inch thickness. With floured 2½-inch cookie cutters, cut the dough into as many cookies as possible. Place the cookies about 1 inch apart on ungreased baking sheets. Refrigerate the scraps before rerolling the dough.

6. Bake the cookies for 12 to 15 minutes, or until they are golden around the edges. Transfer the cookies to a wire rack to cool. Repeat with the remaining dough.

7. In a small bowl, combine the confectioners' sugar with just enough water to make a smooth icing that can be piped. Divide the icing between 2 or more bowls and tint with food colors as desired.

8. To decorate the cookies, spoon the icing into a pastry bag fitted with a small plain tip. Pipe designs onto the cookies as desired. Gently press dragées into the icing. Let the cookies stand until the icing is set.

Makes about 4 dozen cookies

■ **COOKIE BUNDLES**

Bake the same-shape cookie in three different sizes. For a sweet party favor, stack the cookies from largest to smallest and tie them with a ribbon.

· · · · · · · · · ·

Silky Peanut Butter Fudge

This nutty fudge is a wonderful gift for any peanut lover. Keep the pieces layered between sheets of waxed paper.

One 10-ounce package peanut butter-flavored chips

One 14-ounce can sweetened condensed milk

½ cup peanut butter

1. Spray an 8-inch baking pan with nonstick spray.

2. In a heavy saucepan, combine the chips, milk, and peanut butter over low heat. Stir until the peanut butter and chips are melted and smooth. Pour the mixture into the prepared pan and chill for 2 hours.

3. Turn the fudge out onto a cutting board and cut into 1-inch squares. Store in an airtight container up to 3 days.

Makes 64 pieces

Chicken Stew with Tomatoes and Root Vegetables

Get back to your roots! At this nippy time of year, chicken stew, with nourishing root vegetables and a splash of Burgundy, is the ultimate comfort food.

½ teaspoon garlic powder

Salt

Freshly ground pepper

One 4- to 4½-pound chicken, cut into 8 pieces

1 tablespoon butter

2 cups sliced button mushrooms

4 strips bacon, cut into ¼-inch-wide strips

1 medium onion, cut into chunks

2 carrots, peeled and cut into ½-inch cubes

1 parsnip, peeled and cut into ½-inch cubes

1 turnip, peeled and cut into ½-inch cubes

3 garlic cloves, minced

One 28-ounce can whole tomatoes, drained and chopped

One 14½-ounce can chicken stock

1 cup Burgundy

¼ cup chopped fresh parsley, for garnish

1. In a bowl, combine the garlic powder, 1 teaspoon salt, and ½ teaspoon pepper; mix well. Rinse and dry the chicken; season with the salt mixture.

2. In a Dutch oven, melt the butter over medium heat. Add the mushrooms, season with salt and pepper, and cook, stirring occasionally, for 5 to 7 minutes, or until they release their liquid. Remove the mushrooms from the pan and set aside. Add the bacon to the pan and cook for 3 minutes, or until almost crisp. Transfer the bacon to a paper towel–lined plate and set aside.

3. Add the chicken pieces to the Dutch oven, skin side down, and cook for about 8 minutes, or until browned. Turn over and cook for 8 minutes longer, or until browned. Transfer the chicken to a plate.

4. Discard all but 2 tablespoons oil from the Dutch oven. Add the onion and cook for 5 to 7 minutes, or until translucent. Add the cubed carrots, parsnip, and turnip. Season with salt and pepper, cover, and cook for about 10 minutes, or until softened. Add the garlic and cook for 1 minute, or until fragrant. Return the chicken to the pot and add the tomatoes, stock, and wine. Cover and bring to a simmer. Reduce the heat to low and cook for 1 hour, or until the chicken is falling off the bone.

5. Transfer the stew to a deep platter or serving bowl, arranging the chicken pieces skin side up, and garnish with the mushrooms, bacon, and parsley.

Serves 6 to 8

· · · · · · · · · ·

Holiday Potato Chips

These crunchy chips will go faster than Blitzen! Serve them with one or two pesto dips you've bought; we say why make your own dips when there are two billion in the store?

2 pounds russet potatoes

Olive oil, for brushing

Salt, to taste

1. Preheat the oven to 400°F. Line two large baking sheets with parchment paper.

2. With a sharp knife, cut the potatoes into ⅛-inch-thick slices. Arrange the slices on the prepared baking sheets and brush both sides with olive oil. Sprinkle with salt.

3. Bake the chips until golden, 20 to 25 minutes. Transfer to paper towels to drain. Serve the chips in a basket.

Serves 6 to 8

Snowman Cake

Have fun with snowman's fashion accessories. In place of this more formal top hat, give him a pair of cookie earmuffs. Keep his neck warm by bundling him up in a licorice scarf.

MARZIPAN TOP HAT AND NOSE

Black, green, red, and orange paste food coloring

4 tablespoons prepared marzipan

Cornstarch (optional)

CHOCOLATE LAYER CAKE

¾ cup milk, at room temperature

1 tablespoon fresh lemon juice

2 teaspoons vanilla extract

3 ounces unsweetened chocolate, finely chopped

¾ cup boiling water

¾ cup (1 ½ sticks) unsalted butter,
   at room temperature

2 cups sugar

3 large eggs, at room temperature

2 ¼ cups flour

1 ½ teaspoons baking soda

¾ teaspoon baking powder

½ teaspoon salt

½ cup toasted, ground hazelnuts

COCONUT ICING

1 ½ cups (3 sticks) unsalted butter,
   at room temperature

9 cups confectioners' sugar

9 to 12 tablespoons milk

1 tablespoon vanilla extract

¼ teaspoon salt

1 ½ cups sweetened
   shredded coconut,
   finely chopped

About ½ cup raspberry jam

3 cups sweetened shredded coconut

Colored and black gum-drops

2 twigs

2 candy canes

1. Prepare the marzipan top hat and nose 1 to 2 days in advance. Line a baking sheet with parchment paper.

2. Make the top hat: Knead enough black food coloring into 3 tablespoons of the marzipan to tint it deep black. If the marzipan seems very sticky, knead in a little cornstarch. Shape into a ball.

3. On a lightly greased work surface, roll 1 tablespoon of the black marzipan into a ⅛-inch thickness. Use a 2-inch round cookie cutter to cut out a circle. Knead the scraps into the remaining black marzipan.

4. Place the circle onto the prepared baking sheet. Slip 2 straws under the brim to give it a little lift on either side.

5. Roll the remainder of the black marzipan into a 2-inch-long log, slightly tapered at one end. Use your fingers to smooth and slightly depress the top of the wider end to create the top of the hat. Lightly moisten the center of the hat brim and press the top onto it.

6. Make the holly leaves: Knead enough green food coloring into about ½ teaspoon marzipan to tint it green. You can make the leaves bright green or dark green by adjusting the amount of coloring.

7. On a lightly greased work surface, roll out the green marzipan to a 1⁄16-inch thickness. Using a ½-inch cookie cutter, cut out 3 leaves. Using the back of a small paring knife, trace veins on the leaves. Lightly moisten the back of the leaves and press them onto the hat.

8. Make the berries: Knead enough red food coloring into about ¼ teaspoon marzipan to tint it red. Roll tiny pieces of the marzipan into balls. Lightly moisten them with water and press onto the hat.

9. Make the nose: Knead enough orange coloring into 1 teaspoon marzipan to tint it orange. Shape the marzipan into a carrot shape. Place a toothpick in the thick end, which will hold the nose on the cake. Let all the marzipan shapes dry for 1 to 2 days.

10. Make the chocolate cake: Preheat the oven to 350°F. Grease two 4-inch by 2-inch cake pans, two 5-inch by 2-inch cake pans, and two 6-inch by 2-inch cake pans. Line the pans with parchment paper and grease the parchment.

11. Put the milk in a bowl and add the lemon juice to sour it. Add the vanilla. Place the chocolate in a bowl, pour the boiling water over it, and stir until the chocolate has melted. Allow to cool.

12. In the bowl of an electric mixer, beat the butter at high speed until light and smooth, 1 to 2 minutes. Gradually add the sugar, beating at medium speed until the mixture is light and fluffy. Add the eggs one at a time, blending thoroughly and scraping down the sides of the bowl with a rubber spatula after each addition. Add the chocolate mixture and mix just until blended.

13. Sift together the flour, baking soda, baking powder, and salt. With the mixer on low speed, add the flour mixture alternately with the milk mixture to the butter mixture, beginning and ending with the flour, mixing just until combined; scrape down the sides of the bowl frequently. Fold in the hazelnuts.

14. Divide the cake batter among the pans. Bake the small cakes for about 25 minutes, the bigger cakes for about 35 minutes, or until a cake tester inserted in the center comes out clean. Cool the cakes in the pans on wire racks. Remove the cakes from the pans and let cool completely on wire racks. Wrap in plastic wrap and refrigerate overnight.

15. Make the coconut icing: In the bowl of an electric mixer, beat the butter at medium-high speed until very soft and light, about 3 minutes. Reduce the mixer speed to low and gradually add the sugar, 9 tablespoons of the milk, the vanilla, and salt and beat until smooth and fluffy, adding up to 3 tablespoons more milk if necessary. Beat in the coconut. Cover with plastic wrap.

16. Assemble the snowman: Using a serrated knife, cut each cake into 2 layers. Use the domed layers for the top and bottom of each "ball" and flat layers in the middle.

17. In a small saucepan, heat the raspberry jam, stirring, over low heat until smooth.

18. Stack each set of layers, spreading about 1½ tablespoons jam and then ¼ cup of the icing between the layers of the top ball, about 2½ tablespoons jam and ¾ cup icing between the layers of the middle ball, and about 4 tablespoons jam and 1 cup icing between the layers of the bottom ball. Place on a baking sheet and refrigerate for about 30 minutes to firm.

19. Use a serrated knife to shave and better define the balls, rounding the top and bottom edges slightly.

20. Coat the snowman with a thin layer of icing to seal in the crumbs. (If the icing is too dry, beat in a little water.) Refrigerate the cakes for 30 minutes.

21. Place the largest ball in the center of a serving platter. Center the middle ball on it, making sure it is stable. Center the smallest ball on the middle ball, making sure it is stable. Insert a skewer into the top of the snowman all the way to the bottom; trim flush with the top of the cake. Use the remaining icing to to frost the snowman. Gently press the 3 cups coconut into the icing.

22. Use additional coconut icing to attach the decorations. Attach the black gumdrops into the top ball of the snowman to make eyes and a mouth. Attach 2 colored gumdrops each into the middle and bottom balls for buttons. Attach the candy canes where the head meets the middle ball for the bow tie, placing them in opposite directions. Press the twigs into the sides of the snowman for the arms. Press the top hat and nose into place.

Serves 16 to 20

Cranberry-Ginger Punch

Tart, sweet, and bubbly all at once, zingy cranberry punch appeals to grown-ups and children alike. For alternative decorations, float mint leaves or whole raspberries in each cup.

One 11½-ounce can
    cranberry juice
    concentrate,
    thawed
3 cups ginger ale
1 cup seltzer
1 lemon, sliced
    crosswise and
    seeded

In a large pitcher, combine the cranberry juice concentrate and ginger ale; stir to combine. Add the seltzer and lemon slices and gently stir. Serve immediately in ice-filled cups or glasses.

Serves 6 to 8

■ PUNCH WITH A KICK

For adults, make up a separate recipe and pour in a bottle of Champagne.

Garlic Toasts with Olive Tapenade

The earthy taste of our customized tapenade toasts makes this fast, easy hors d'oeuvres so popular at parties.

One 6-ounce jar green olive tapenade
8 to 10 garlic cloves, halved
¼ cup olive oil
1 small thin baguette, cut into ¼-inch slices

1. Preheat the broiler. Spoon the tapenade into a small serving bowl.

2. In a small saucepan, heat the garlic and oil over low heat for 4 minutes, or until just fragrant; do not let the garlic burn. Remove from the heat.

3. Brush the baguette slices on both sides with the garlic oil. Place the slices on an ungreased baking sheet. Broil the toasts 4 inches from the heat for 1 minute, or until golden brown. Turn the slices over and broil for about another minute, or until golden brown.

4. Place the bowl of tapenade in the middle of a serving plate or platter. Arrange the toasts on the platter. Serve immediately.

Serves 4

Santa's Pantry

Don't panic when the doorbell rings unexpectedly! Instead, be prepared with the basics for an impromptu party. Stock the pantry with seltzer and juices. Lay away one or two bottles of wine, some chips and dip, and a jar of olives. If you have ice cream, pound cake, and berries in the freezer, you have dessert!

Spinach, Cheese, and Steak Pinwheels

Promote cheese steaks from everyday to absolutely special. This perfect presentation suggests that you slaved for hours over a hot stove. The pinwheels really take only minutes to put together.

1½ pounds flank steak

Salt and freshly ground pepper, to taste

¼ small bunch spinach (tough stems removed), halved lengthwise

About eight ⅛-inch-thick slices Monterey Jack cheese

1. Preheat the broiler. Lightly oil an 8-inch cast-iron skillet.

2. Place the steak on a cutting board and sprinkle with salt and pepper on both sides. Slice the meat crosswise against the grain into 1-inch-wide slices.

3. Cover each slice with a layer of spinach leaves and a layer of cheese, leaving a ¼-inch border at one short end. Carefully roll up the meat, starting at the short end that is covered with spinach and cheese, and secure the roll with a toothpick. Place the rolls in the prepared skillet. Broil 4 inches from the heat for 6 to 8 minutes, or until nicely browned. The temperature on instant-read thermometer will register 125°F for medium-rare when inserted into the thickest part of the meat. Transfer the pinwheels to a cutting board and let them rest for 5 minutes.

4. Remove the toothpicks, transfer the pinwheels to plates, and serve.

Serves 4

Wild Rice with Herbs

Wild rice can be breathtakingly expensive; prepackaged long-grain and wild rice mixes are an economical, delicious alternative.

Two 6-ounce packages long-grain and wild rice mixture

1 tablespoon chopped fresh chives

2 teaspoons chopped fresh parsley

1 teaspoon chopped fresh sage

Prepare the rice according to the package directions. Just before serving, stir in the herbs. Transfer to a serving bowl and serve immediately.

Serves 4

Peas with Almonds

To keep things interesting, a handful of slivered almonds intensifies the sweetness of the peas and adds crunch to this simple dish.

2 tablespoons butter

2 cups frozen tiny peas

¼ cup slivered almonds

Salt and freshly ground pepper, to taste

Orange zest, for garnish

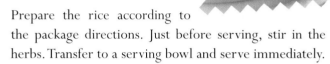

In a medium saucepan, melt the butter over medium heat. Add the peas and almonds and cook, stirring, for about 5 minutes, or until the peas are tender. Remove from the heat and season with salt and pepper. Transfer to a serving dish, garnish with orange zest, and serve immediately.

Serves 4

Chocolate-Amaretto Cheesecake

The little black dress of the baking world, cheesecake can be dressed up or down; it can take on most any accessory from chocolate curls to a sprinkle of nuts. In this case, we flavored the cheesecake with chocolate and splashes of amaretto for a rich taste.

¼ cup (½ stick) butter, melted

Half a 9-ounce box chocolate wafers, crushed

1 pound cream cheese, at room temperature

½ cup sugar

2 large eggs, at room temperature

1 teaspoon vanilla extract

Pinch of salt

4 ounces semisweet chocolate, melted and cooled

2 tablespoons amaretto or other almond-flavored liqueur

1 teaspoon almond extract

4 ounces white chocolate

Chocolate twigs, for garnish

1. Preheat the oven to 350°F. Wrap the bottom of the outside of a 6- by 2½-inch springform pan in a large sheet of foil so the foil comes halfway up the side.

2. In a small bowl, combine the butter and chocolate wafer crumbs. Gently press the mixture into the bottom of the prepared pan. Bake for 10 minutes. Transfer the pan to a wire rack to cool. Leave the oven on.

3. In the large bowl of an electric mixer, at medium-high speed, beat the cream cheese until it is light and fluffy. Scrape down the side of the bowl, add the sugar, and beat until the mixture is well blended. Scrape down the side of the bowl and add the eggs one at a time, beating until blended. Beat in the vanilla and salt. Transfer half the mixture to a medium bowl.

4. Beat the semisweet chocolate into one of the bowls of cheese mixture, mixing until combined. Pour into the prepared pan and smooth the top with a spatula.

5. Beat the amaretto and almond extract into the remaining cheese mixture. Slowly pour the mixture on the chocolate layer. Smooth the top.

6. Bake the cheesecake for 45 to 50 minutes, or until almost set (it will not be completely set in the middle). Prop the oven door open with a wooden spoon. Turn the oven off and let the cheesecake remain there for 1 hour longer.

7. Remove the cheesecake from the oven and run a knife around the pan edge to loosen it. Transfer the cake in the pan to a wire rack and let cool completely. Cover with plastic wrap and refrigerate overnight.

8. Melt the white chocolate in the top of a double boiler over simmering water. When it is smooth, pour the chocolate onto an ungreased baking sheet. With a spatula, spread the chocolate into a thin layer. Refrigerate until the chocolate is set, at least 30 minutes.

9. Remove the white chocolate from the refrigerator and let sit for 10 minutes. Pull a metal spatula or long knife along the chocolate to create curls and shavings. Store the curls in the refrigerator.

10. Let the cheesecake sit at room temperature for at least 30 minutes before serving. Remove the side of the pan and transfer the cake to a serving platter. Garnish with chocolate curls and chocolate twigs.

11. Cut the cake with a large knife dipped in hot water and wiped clean between each slice.

Serves 4 to 6

■ SEASON'S GREETINGS

Spoon melted chocolate into a pastry bag fitted with a small round tip. In your best penmanship, pipe "Happy Holidays!" around the rim of the dessert platter.

Turkey Pot Pie

There's something about the word "pie" that is immediately appealing. Which would you rather have: leftovers or pie?

4 tablespoons (½ stick) butter

2 tablespoons flour

2 ¼ cups chicken stock

½ cup heavy cream

Salt and freshly
    ground pepper,
    to taste

1 cup chopped onions

2 garlic cloves, minced

2 cups sliced button
    mushrooms

1 cup sliced carrots

1 medium potato, peeled
    and cut into ½-inch chunks

3 cups shredded or chopped cooked turkey

¼ cup frozen corn

Half a 17½-ounce package puff pastry (1 sheet),
    thawed according to package instructions

1 large egg, beaten

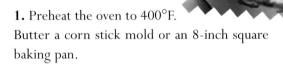

1. In a medium saucepan, melt 2 tablespoons butter over medium heat. Whisk in the flour until the mixture is bubbling. Gradually whisk in 1¼ cups stock and the cream. Bring to a simmer and cook, whisking constantly, until the mixture has thickened. Remove from the heat, season with salt and pepper, and set aside.

2. In a large saucepan, melt the remaining 2 tablespoons butter over medium heat. Add the onions, season with salt and pepper, and cook, stirring frequently, for 3 to 5 minutes, or until the onions are golden. Add the garlic, and immediately stir in the mushrooms, carrots, and potato. Add the remaining ½ cup stock and cook, stirring occasionally, for 10 minutes, or until the carrots and potatoes begin to soften. Stir in the turkey, corn, and sauce and season with salt and pepper. Transfer the mixture to a 13- by 9-inch baking dish.

3. Preheat the oven to 350°F. On a lightly floured surface, with a floured rolling pin, roll out the puff pastry to a ¹⁄₁₆-inch thickness; trim to a 14- by 10-inch rectangle. Brush the edges of the baking dish with the beaten egg.

4. Roll the pastry onto a rolling pin and unroll over the filling. Press down and crimp the edges to seal. Cut an 'X' in the top of the pastry as a steam vent.

5. Bake the pie for 40 to 50 minutes, or until the top is golden brown. Let rest for 5 minutes before serving.

Serves 4 to 6

∙∙∙∙∙∙∙∙∙∙

Red Pepper Corn Sticks

Serve these golden corn bread sticks piping hot with butter and honey or a Southwestern jalapeño jelly. You'll always wish you'd made a second batch.

1 large egg

⅓ cup milk

One 8½-ounce package corn
    muffin mix

¼ cup frozen corn, thawed

¼ cup diced red bell pepper

1 tablespoon minced
    fresh dill

1. Preheat the oven to 400°F. Butter a corn stick mold or an 8-inch square baking pan.

2. In a large bowl, combine the egg and milk, mixing well. Add the muffin mix and stir just to combine. Stir in the corn, red pepper, and dill. Let sit for 3 minutes.

3. Pour the batter into the prepared pan. Bake for 15 to 25 minutes, or until golden brown on top and a toothpick inserted in the center comes out clean. Let cool for 5 minutes on a wire rack.

4. Remove from the pan. Serve as sticks or cut into 2- by 4-inch slices.

Serves 4 to 6

Peppermint Hot Chocolate

Peppermint stick stirrers add a festive touch to hot chocolate. But the minty taste really comes from a secret ingredient—mint extract.

½ pound high-quality semisweet chocolate, coarsely chopped

1 quart milk

1 teaspoon mint extract

6 peppermint sticks, for garnish

Whipped heavy cream, for garnish

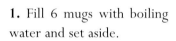

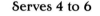

1. Fill 6 mugs with boiling water and set aside.

2. In a medium nonstick saucepan, combine the chopped chocolate and milk. Heat over medium heat, whisking constantly, until the chocolate has melted and steam begins to rise from the pan; do not let the mixture reach a boil. Remove from the heat and stir in the extract.

3. Discard the water from the mugs and pour the hot chocolate into the hot mugs. Garnish with peppermint sticks and whipped cream.

Serves 4 to 6

▦ SPICY MEXICAN HOT CHOCOLATE

For a hotter version, substitute dashes of cinnamon and chile powder for the mint extract. Sprinkle the chocolate with nutmeg and use cinnamon sticks as stirrers.

Cherry S'mores

Why are these toasty desserts reserved for summer? In all their gooey chocolate glory, s'mores take the chill right off the coldest winter day.

16 graham crackers, broken crosswise in half

Four 1.5-ounce chocolate bars, broken into quarters

About 5 tablespoons chopped dried cherries

16 large marshmallows

1. Preheat the broiler. Line a baking sheet with foil.

2. Place half the graham crackers on the prepared baking sheet. Top each cracker with 1 chocolate piece, 1 teaspoon cherries, and 1 marshmallow. Broil the s'mores for 1 minute, or until the marshmallows turn golden. Immediately top each with a remaining graham crackers. Pile the s'mores on a platter and serve immediately.

Serves 4 to 6

Santa's Pantry

To give parties a crowning touch, pull out all the stops with dessert. While you're in the kitchen brewing coffee, create a batch of chocolate-coated spoons. It's easy: melt some chocolate over a double boiler. Dip teaspoons into the chocolate, then into colored sugar crystals. Let the spoons sit on waxed paper for 5 minutes to set.

Raspberry-Orange Vodka

We love the make-ahead possibilities of this recipe. You can do most of the work the weekend before your party, and then bottle your final creations the day before.

Two 12-ounce bags frozen raspberries, thawed

Zest of ½ orange, removed with a vegetable peeler

About 3 cups vodka

1½ cups water

1 cup sugar

1. Crush the berries in a bowl. Transfer to a jar, add the orange zest and 2 cups vodka, and shake well to mix. Add more vodka if necessary to cover the fruit. Seal tightly and refrigerate for up to 1 week.

2. Combine the water and sugar in a small saucepan and heat over medium heat, stirring, until the sugar dissolves. Set aside to cool completely.

3. Place a large sieve lined with double layer of cheese-cloth over a bowl with a spout. Strain the vodka into the bowl. Squeeze the cheesecloth to release all the liquid; discard the solids. Strain the vodka once or twice again through clean cheesecloth.

4. Stir the remaining 1 cup vodka and the sugar syrup into the strained vodka. Pour the vodka into a bottle and seal tightly.

Makes about 5 cups

Stuffed Shrimp

Everyone loves shrimp—even kids. We've stuffed them with bread crumbs and pancetta, but you might prefer bacon.

24 jumbo shrimp in the shell

1 tablespoon vegetable oil

1 cup finely chopped onions

Salt and freshly ground
pepper, to taste

½ pound pancetta,
finely chopped

1 large garlic clove, minced

1 cup Italian-flavor bread
crumbs

2 large eggs, lightly beaten

2½ tablespoons chopped fresh parsley

1. With kitchen shears, split the shrimp shells open down the back. With a paring knife, make a slit lengthwise down each shrimp from the tail to the head, cutting half to three-quarters of the way through the shrimp. Remove the dark vein and rinse the shrimp under cold running water. Pat the shrimp dry, place on a plate, cover, and refrigerate.

2. In a medium skillet, heat the oil over medium-high heat. Add the onions, season with salt and pepper, and cook for 3 minutes, or until softened. Add the pancetta and cook 5 minutes. Add the garlic and cook 30 seconds. Transfer the mixture to a medium bowl and add the bread crumbs, eggs, parsley, and pepper, mixing well.

3. Place a heaping spoonful of the filling in the opening in each shrimp, pressing down to compress. Cover and refrigerate for 1 hour.

4. Preheat the oven to 425°F. Grease a baking sheet.

5. Place the shrimp, stuffing side up and 1 inch apart, on the prepared baking sheet. Bake 5 minutes, or until the shrimp are pink and the stuffing is lightly browned.

Serves 8

Pork Wraps with Salsa

Pork and beans never looked (or tasted) so sophisticated. Because these little packets are wraps, they make even the amateur cook look quite accomplished.

1 teaspoon chile powder

½ teaspoon garlic powder

1 teaspoon salt

Freshly ground pepper, to taste

1¼ pounds boneless pork chops

2 tablespoons vegetable oil

4 cups medium-hot salsa

1½ cups canned black beans, rinsed

1½ cups frozen corn, thawed

Three 12½-inch tomato-flavored flour tortillas

9 to 12 romaine lettuce leaves, center ribs removed

1. In a small bowl, combine the chile powder, garlic powder, salt, and pepper. Sprinkle the pork chops on both sides with the seasoning mixture.

2. In a large skillet, heat the oil over medium heat. Add the pork chops and cook for 3 to 5 minutes on each side, or until no longer pink inside. Transfer the pork chops to a cutting board and let rest for 5 minutes, then cut into thin slices.

3. In a large bowl, combine 3 cups salsa with the beans and corn; mix well.

4. Lay 1 tortilla on a work surface and arrange 3 or 4 lettuce leaves on top, leaving a 1-inch border all around. Place one-third of the pork and one-third of the salsa mixture on the lettuce. Roll the tortilla up; moisten the edge of the tortilla with water and press to seal. Set the wrap seam side down on a plate. Repeat with the remaining ingredients. Cover and refrigerate for 15 to 30 minutes.

5. With a serrated knife, trim the ends from each tortilla, then cut into ½-inch slices. Skewer each slice with a toothpick to hold it together and place cut side up on a serving plate. Serve with a bowl of the remaining salsa.

Serves 8

....

Chicken Liver and Bacon Wraps

Beware! These irresistible morsels have an addictive quality. Finger food at its most satisfying, they take almost as little time to make as they do to eat.

½ teaspoon garlic powder

½ teaspoon salt

12 chicken livers, trimmed and halved

12 slices bacon, cut crosswise in half

Freshly ground pepper, to taste

1. Soak 24 toothpicks in water for 30 minutes.

2. Preheat the broiler.

3. In a small bowl, combine the garlic powder and salt. Sprinkle the chicken livers with half the salt mixture. Wrap ½ slice bacon around each chicken liver half and secure with a toothpick. Sprinkle the wraps with the remaining salt mixture and season with pepper. Arrange on a broiling pan.

4. Broil the wraps 4 to 6 inches from the heat for 5 to 7 minutes, or until the bacon begins to crisp. Turn over and broil for 5 to 7 minutes longer, or until the chicken livers are no longer pink inside and the bacon is crispy. Transfer the hors d'oeuvres to a platter and let cool slightly before serving.

Serves 8

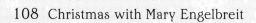

Beggars' Purses with Surprise Fillings

Think of it as hors d'oeuvres roulette. From the outside, you can't tell what a beggar's purse might hold—even if it's sweet or savory. So prepare for adventure.

RUM-RAISIN FILLING

¾ cup raisins

¼ cup rum

2 cinnamon sticks

CHEDDAR, POTATO, AND PEA FILLING

½ cup mashed potatoes

¼ cup frozen peas, thawed

3 tablespoons shredded Cheddar cheese

Salt and freshly ground pepper, to taste

CHOCOLATE-WALNUT FILLING

2 ounces semisweet chocolate, finely chopped

3 tablespoons heavy cream

2 tablespoons ground walnuts

BEEF AND CARROT FILLING

1 tablespoon vegetable oil

2 tablespoons minced onion

¼ pound ground beef

2 tablespoons shredded carrot

Salt and freshly ground pepper, to taste

1 garlic clove, minced

Two 17½-ounce packages filo dough, thawed according to package directions

1 cup (2 sticks) butter, melted

1. Make the rum-raisin filling: Place the raisins in a medium bowl. In a small saucepan, heat the rum with the cinnamon sticks over low heat just until hot. Pour the rum over the raisins. Cover the bowl and let the raisins plump for 30 minutes.

2. Preheat the oven to 400°F. Lightly butter 3 large baking sheets. Cut sixty-four 6- by ½-inch strips of foil.

3. Make the cheddar, potato, and pea filling: In a large bowl, combine the potatoes, peas, cheddar, salt, and pepper, and stir until well mixed. Cover and set aside.

4. Make the chocolate-walnut filling: Place the chocolate in a medium bowl. In a small saucepan, heat the cream over low heat until simmering. Immediately pour the cream over the chocolate and let sit for 1 minute. Stir the chocolate and cream until smooth. Stir in the walnuts. Cover and set aside.

5. Make the beef and carrot filling: In a large skillet, heat the oil over medium heat. Add the onion and cook until translucent. Add the ground beef and crumble with a wooden spoon. Add the carrot, season with salt and pepper, and cook for 3 to 5 minutes, or until the beef is browned. Add the garlic and cook for 1 minute, or until fragrant. Transfer to a medium bowl and set aside.

6. Lay one sheet of filo on a work surface. (Keep the rest of the filo sheets completely covered with plastic wrap and a damp towel while you work.) With a pastry brush, brush the sheet with melted butter. Cut the sheet crosswise in half. Fold each half crosswise in half and then crosswise in half again. Spoon 2 teaspoons of a filling onto the center of each filo square. Gather the four corners of the filo over the filling and pinch the top. Wrap strips of foil around the neck of the purse and twist the foil to seal it. Transfer to the prepared baking sheet and brush with melted butter. Repeat with the remaining filo and filling.

7. Bake the purses for 20 to 25 minutes, or until golden and crisp. Set the pan on a wire rack to cool slightly, then remove the foil strips. Transfer to a platter.

Serves 8 to 12

Baby Apple Pies

Baked in a paper bag tent, these little pies are browned to perfection. Have them just coming out of the oven when guests arrive, so that their heavenly aroma curls into every corner of the house.

Dough for two 9-inch pie crusts

8 brown paper bags

4 medium Jonathan or

Winesap apples

2 teaspoons fresh lemon juice

1 cup sugar

½ cup plus 2 tablespoons

flour

1 teaspoon ground cinnamon

¼ teaspoon ground nutmeg

½ cup (1 stick) cold butter

1. Preheat the oven to 400°F. Have ready eight 2½-inch tartlet pans with removable bottoms.

2. Lay a paper bag on a work surface and invert a tart pan onto the bag, toward the bottom. Trace the outline of the pan onto the bag. With scissors, cut out the circle from half the bag. Repeat with the remaining bags. Set aside the bags and circles.

3. Cut the dough into eight 5-inch rounds. Line each of the tartlet pans with a round of dough and trim even with the rim. Refrigerate the tartlet pans.

4. Peel and core the apples and cut into ¼-inch dice. Place in a large bowl and toss with lemon juice.

5. In a small bowl, combine ½ cup sugar, 2 tablespoons flour, the cinnamon, and nutmeg. Sprinkle over the apples and toss to coat. Divide the apples evenly among the tartlet pans.

6. In a small bowl, combine the remaining ½ cup sugar and ½ cup flour. With a pastry blender or two knives, cut in the butter until the mixture resembles coarse crumbs. Sprinkle evenly over the pies.

7. Place a pie in a bag, centering it under the cut out circle. Fold the top of the bag over and staple closed. Place the circle on top of the hole. Repeat with remaining pies and bags. Place the bags on baking sheets.

8. Bake for 30 minutes. Remove the circles and bake for 30 minutes longer, or until the tops are lightly browned. Carefully remove the pies from the bags and set on wire racks to cool for 20 minutes. Remove the sides of the pans and serve the pies warm or at room temperature.

Serves 8

Grape Punch

The kids will love to help make this punch, which you'll need to start the day before the party. Cool it overnight in the refrigerator or on the porch.

4 clementines

48 whole cloves

2 quarts white grape juice

8 cinnamon sticks

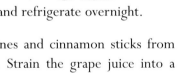

1. Pierce each clementine with 12 cloves. Place the grape juice, clementines, and cinnamon sticks in a large bowl. Cover with plastic wrap and refrigerate overnight.

2. Remove the clementines and cinnamon sticks from the grape juice; discard. Strain the grape juice into a large pitcher and serve.

Serves 8

Santa's Pantry

Bring along a jar or two of your summer fruit preserves as a hostess gift. Of course if your kitchen is as hectic as ours, you didn't put up summer fruit, but it's not too late. Homemade applesauce is delicious and fast to prepare: It's a savior. Cook seeded apples in water till soft; blend and flavor with nutmeg. Voilá!

Arugula, Radicchio, and Endive Salad

Tender, spicy green arugula, sweet and crunchy white and light green endive, and brilliant ruby-colored radicchio capture the colors of the season on your plate.

5 cups arugula

7 heads endive, leaves separated and trimmed

1½ heads radicchio, leaves separated and trimmed

1½ cups bottled poppy seed dressing

1. Slice or tear the arugula into bite-size pieces and place in a large serving bowl. Cut the endive into ¼-inch slices and add to the bowl. Cut the radicchio into very thin slices and add to the bowl. Cover the bowl with a moistened paper towel and refrigerate until ready to serve. Can be made up to 4 hours ahead.

2. To serve, toss the salad until combined. Pour the dressing over the salad, toss to coat, and serve.

Serves 12 to 14

Spicy Pineapple Glazed Ham

This sweet and spicy ham will be the centerpiece of your buffet. If desired, spike the ham with cloves before baking.

One 14-pound fully cooked bone-in smoked ham

One 20-ounce can crushed pineapple, drained

½ cup packed dark brown sugar

1 tablespoon dry mustard

1½ teaspoons ground red pepper

1½ teaspoons chile powder

1. Preheat the oven to 325°F.

2. Remove the skin and trim all but a ¼-inch layer of fat from the ham. Place the ham on a rack in a roasting pan and bake for 1½ hours.

3. Meanwhile, in a large bowl, combine the pineapple, sugar, mustard, red pepper, and chile powder, stirring until blended.

4. Spoon the pineapple mixture over the ham. Return it to the oven and bake about 45 minutes longer, or until an instant read thermometer registers 135°F when inserted into the thickest part of the ham. Transfer the ham to a cutting board and let rest for 15 minutes before carving.

Serves 12 to 14

Sweet Potato Casserole

Children will be lured by the puff of toasted marshmallows that crowns this tasty casserole, known here in the heart of the country as "The World's Best Sweet Potato Dish."

4 cups mashed cooked sweet potatoes

2 cups packed brown sugar

1 cup (2 sticks) butter, melted

¼ cup honey

¼ teaspoon salt

2 cups sweetened
   condensed milk

4 teaspoons ground
   cinnamon

2 cups pecans,
   chopped

20 large
   marshmallows

1. Preheat the oven to 375°F. Butter a 13- by 9-inch baking dish and set aside.

2. In a large bowl, with a wooden spoon, beat the potatoes, sugar, butter, honey, and salt until thoroughly combined. Add the condensed milk and cinnamon and mix well. Stir in the pecans.

3. Spoon the mixture into the prepared baking dish. Bake for 30 minutes.

4. Remove the casserole from the oven and evenly place the marshmallows on the top. Return to the oven and bake for 10 minutes longer, or until the marshmallows are golden brown and slightly melted. Let stand for 5 minutes before serving.

Serves 12 to 14

■ GINGER SWEET POTATO CASSEROLE

Stud the top with candied ginger instead of marshmallows for a jewel-like effect and a more sophisticated taste.

Broccoli with Pine Nuts and Garlic

Firm, tight heads and crisp stalks are the signs that you've got an exceptional head of broccoli on your hands. For a twist, mix traditional green and new varieties of broccoli, including chartreuse and purple.

5 pounds broccoli, about 4 bunches, rinsed

⅔ cup water

3 tablespoons vegetable oil

2 to 3 garlic cloves, minced

½ cup pine nuts, toasted

Salt, to taste

1. Cut the florets off the broccoli and place in a large bowl; discard the stems.

2. In a large skillet, cook ⅓ cup water and one-half of the broccoli over medium-high heat. Cook, tossing frequently with tongs, until bright green and just tender, about 7 minutes. Transfer the broccoli to a large serving bowl, cover with plastic wrap, and set aside. Continue cooking the remaining broccoli.

3. Wipe the skillet dry and heat the vegetable oil over low heat. Add the garlic and sauté for 2 to 3 minutes, or until light golden brown and fragrant. Remove from the heat and pour the garlic oil over the broccoli.

4. Sprinkle the broccoli with the pine nuts and salt and toss to combine. Serve immediately.

Serves 12 to 14

Peach-Scented Eggnog

Everyone loves eggnog, but even classic holiday fare needs a little creative tweaking from time to time. We've given ours a filip of peach schnapps, but you could choose a chocolate—or almond— flavored liqueur just as easily.

9 large eggs, separated
6 tablespoons sugar
2 quarts plus 1 cup milk
3/4 cup peach schnapps
3/4 cup dark rum
1 1/2 teaspoons vanilla extract
Ground nutmeg, for garnish

1. In a large bowl, whisk the egg yolks with the sugar until well blended. Whisk in the milk, schnapps, rum, and vanilla until well combined.

2. In the medium bowl of an electric mixer, beat the egg whites at medium-high speed until soft peaks form. Fold the egg whites into the egg yolk mixture.

3. Transfer the eggnog to a serving bowl and sprinkle with nutmeg. The eggnog can be chilled for up to 1 hour before serving.

Serves 12 to 14

Panna Cotta with Strawberry Sauce

Here is a silky, eggless custard that any cook in Italy is proud to serve as holiday dessert.

3 cups milk
3/4 ounce unflavored gelatin
1 1/2 quarts heavy cream
1 1/2 cups granulated sugar
4 teaspoons vanilla extract
1 cup frozen strawberries, thawed
2 tablespoons confectioners' sugar
1/2 teaspoon grated lemon zest
1 tablespoon lemon juice
1 cup sweetened shredded coconut, toasted
Mint sprigs, for garnish

1. Place 1 cup milk in a medium saucepan and sprinkle the gelatin over it. Let sit for 5 minutes.

2. Set the pan over low heat and cook, stirring constantly, until the gelatin dissolves. Add the remaining 2 cups milk, the cream, and the granulated sugar. Cook over medium heat, stirring, until steam rises but the mixture has not reached a boil. Turn off the heat, cover, and let sit for 15 minutes. Stir in the vanilla.

3. Divide the mixture between fourteen 6-ounce custard cups. Refrigerate until set, at least 6 hours or overnight.

4. Put the strawberries in a blender. Add the confectioners' sugar, lemon zest and juice; blend to puree.

5. To serve, dip the bottom of each custard cup in hot water for 5 to 10 seconds, then invert a dessert plate over the cup and invert the custard onto the plate.

6. Drizzle the strawberry sauce around each custard. Sprinkle toasted coconut over the custards and garnish with mint sprigs. Serve immediately.

Serves 14

Buttermilk Biscuits with Ham and Chutney

Flaky, rich biscuits are a dandy complement to spicy ham. Keep them moist with sweet chutney.

2 cups flour

1½ teaspoons baking powder

½ teaspoon baking soda

½ teaspoon salt

¼ cup vegetable shortening

¾ cup buttermilk

One 9½-ounce jar cranberry chutney

16 slices Spicy Pineapple Glazed Ham (page 111)

1. Preheat the oven to 450°F.

2. In a large bowl, combine the flour, baking powder, baking soda, and salt. With a pastry blender or two knives, cut in the shortening until the mixture resembles coarse crumbs. Add the buttermilk, stirring just until the dry ingredients are evenly moistened; do not overmix.

3. On a lightly floured surface, knead the dough just until it comes together smoothly, about 8 times. With a floured rolling pin, roll the dough into a ¾-inch-thick round. With a floured 2½-inch biscuit cutter, cut out as many biscuits as possible. Place the biscuits 1 inch apart on an ungreased baking sheet. Gather and reroll the trimmings and cut out more biscuits.

4. Bake the biscuits for 12 to 14 minutes, or until light golden brown. Transfer to a wire rack to cool.

5. Slice the biscuits crosswise in half. Spoon 1 to 2 tablespoons chutney onto the bottom half of each biscuit. Top with 1 or 2 slices of ham and place the biscuit top on the ham. Serve immediately.

Serves 8

Sweet Potato Pancakes

Serve these elegant pancakes with a dollop of sour cream and a side of applesauce for an even bigger burst of flavor.

2 tablespoons butter

½ cup finely chopped scallions

5 cups mashed sweet potatoes

1 cup crumbled blue cheese

2 large eggs, lightly beaten

½ teaspoon chile powder

1¼ teaspoons salt

1½ cups Italian-flavored bread crumbs

Vegetable oil, for frying

1. In a small skillet, melt the butter over medium heat. Add the scallions and cook for 3 to 5 minutes, or until softened. Remove from the heat.

2. In a large bowl, combine the scallions, potatoes, blue cheese, eggs, chile powder, and salt, mixing well.

3. Place the bread crumbs on a large plate. With your hands, form about ¼ cup of the potato mixture at a time into flat patties. Dredge each patty in the bread crumbs, turning to coat. Place the patties on a baking sheet, cover and refrigerate for 30 minutes.

4. Preheat the oven to 200°F. In a large skillet, heat 3 tablespoons vegetable oil over medium heat. Add up to 4 patties; do not crowd the pan. Cook the patties, turning only once, for 3 to 5 minutes on each side, or until lightly browned. Transfer the pancakes to a paper towel–lined plate and keep warm in the oven. Continue with the remaining patties, adding more oil to the skillet as necessary. Serve immediately.

Serves 8

Almond-Plum Mini Cakes

Put in your thumb and pull out a plum! Crowned with juicy fruits, these little cakes make a colorful and sweet holiday treat.

4 purple plums, pitted and cut into eighths

1½ cups flour

1 teaspoon baking powder

½ teaspoon salt

1 cup (2 sticks) butter, at room temperature

1 cup sugar

3 large eggs, at room temperature

2 teaspoons vanilla extract

½ cup ground almonds

1. Preheat the oven to 350°F. Lightly grease and flour 12 muffin cups.

2. Place 2 or 3 slices of plum, skin side down, in the bottom of each muffin cup.

3. In a small bowl, whisk together the flour, baking powder, and salt. Set aside.

4. In the large bowl of an electric mixer, beat the butter at medium speed until light and fluffy. Add the sugar and beat until combined. Add the eggs one at a time, beating well after each addition. Add the vanilla. At low speed, add half the flour mixture, beating just until combined. Add the remaining flour mixture, beating just until combined. Stir in the almonds.

5. Gently fill each muffin cup about two-thirds full with batter, easing the batter between the plums. Bake for 35 minutes, or until a toothpick inserted in the centers comes out clean. Run a small knife around the sides of each cake and transfer the pan to a wire rack to cool for 10 minutes.

6. Invert the pan to remove the cakes. Serve the cakes upside-down.

Serves 8

Eggnog Shakes

Is it a beverage or a dessert? You decide. Eggnog shakes go great with savories, and they're delicious enough to enjoy on their own.

4 cups Peach-Scented Eggnog (page 113)

4 cups chopped thawed frozen peaches

1 pint vanilla ice cream

Ground nutmeg, for garnish

In a blender, combine the eggnog, peaches, and ice cream in batches and blend until smooth. Pour into mugs, garnish with nutmeg, and serve immediately.

Serves 8

▧ RASPBERRY AND PEACH EGGNOG SHAKES

If desired, substitute 4 cups thawed frozen raspberries for the frozen peaches. The taste will be slightly more tart, and the color will be like a Caribbean sunset!

WORKSHOP

Hard work is never easy—so who needs it?

But it wouldn't be Christmas without those handmade presents. We've put on our thinking caps and come up with some terrific surprises. Whether you like to sew, to paint, or to glue, you'll find directions here for a great gift for everybody on your list. If you do enjoy the fuss, there are a couple real challenges. Don't forget a present or two for yourself!

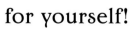 ## Santa's Workshop

For the projects in this section, have the following general supplies on hand.

• Scissors	• Craft knife	• Fine-tip marker
• Sewing, embroidery and upholstery needles and thread	• Cutting surface	• Straight pins
	• Ruler and tape measure	• Iron and ironing board
• Sewing machine	• Paper and pencil	• Hot-glue gun

Velvet Fruit

Real fruit exists to be eaten, but you create these plush velvet ones to be tree ornaments, centerpieces, curtain tie-backs, and decorations for gifts. For keepsake party favors, embroider each with guests' initials.

Supplies for one apple, one pear, and some cherries

Velvet fruit templates, page 134, 135

½ yard each gold, silver, and red cotton velvet

Polyester fiberfill

2 to 3 dozen gold or white seed beads

2 to 3 dozen gold or silver sequins

Brown florist wire stems for apples or pears

3-inch lengths grapevines for cherry stems

Green velvet leaves with wire stems, one per fruit

1. Photocopy the fruit patterns (the patterns are shown actual size) onto paper and cut out.

2. For each piece of fruit, cut out three pattern pieces in velvet. Pin the three pieces of velvet together with right sides facing, allowing ¼" seams.

3. Use a sewing machine or hand stitch the velvet pattern pieces together with coordinating thread, allowing ¼" seams. Leave an opening for turning. With scissors, clip the outer edges of the curves.

4. To simulate drops of dew, sew sets of seed beads and sequins to the sides of the apple and pear.

5. Turn the right sides out, and stuff with fiberfill. Slip-stitch the bottom opening together to close.

6. To shape the apple and the cherries, insert a threaded upholstery needle through the center of each piece of fruit from the top through to the bottom, then back through to the top. Pull the thread tight enough to give the piece of fruit a pleasing shape. Gently manipulate the filling inside to make the fruit appear asymmetrical and slightly off-balance.

7. Tuck the fruit stems into the stitching at the top of the fruits; glue in place. Working in sets of 2 or three, glue the cherries together at the tops of their stems.

8. To attach the leaves, wrap their wire stems around the tops of the fruit stems.

■ FASHION PLATES TAKE NOTE

Cherries look terrific attached to hair clips. Glue them to a pinback and they'll spiff up a coat or sweater. We've made them with cotton velvet from the fabric shop, but think how fabulous they'd be if you had some scraps of vintage silk velvets. You can make strawberries, bananas, watermelons—whatever your palette desires.

Transfer Pillow

Commemorate a favorite photo or display kids' artwork on a transfer-print pillow. And your originals stay intact!

Supplies for 1 pillow

> Photographs or illustrations
> ½ yard white cotton fabric
> ½ yard black and white check fabric for backing
> 2 yards ½" black and white checked ribbon
> Four 1¼" large buttons
> One 16" x 16" pillow form

1. At the local copy shop, have your images duplicated onto transfer paper.

2. For a 16" pillow, cut a 17" square from both the white and the checked fabric.

3. With an iron, following the transfer-paper instructions for heat setting, transfer the artwork to the white fabric.

4. Pin the ribbon borders into place about 2" from the edge of the fabric, crossing the ribbons at the corners. Machine stitch along each edge of the ribbons.

5. Sew on the buttons where the ribbons cross.

6. With the right sides facing, allowing ½" seams, sew the front and back together. Leave at least half of one side open to stuff in the pillow form.

7. Turn the fabric right-side-out and insert the pillow form. Slip-stitch the open edge closed.

Cell Phone Holders

Make a glamorous cell phone holder for Mom; make a teenager's funky! Get the dimensions of the phone first.

Supplies for Mom's

> Cell phone holder pattern, page 135
> 12" x 16" red toile fabric
> 24" red seed-bead trim
> 1 yard red cording
>   for strap
> One 3" red tassel

Supplies for teenager's

> Cell phone holder pattern,
>   page 135
> 12" x 16" silver sparkle
>   denim
> 24" silver seed-bead trim
> 1 yard silver cording
> 4 silver beads in graduating sizes
> 22 small silver beads
> Four 7mm blue plastic glue-on rhinestones

1. This pattern is for a standard size cell phone, but you can adjust the dimensions of the pattern as needed. Photocopy the patterns to actual size and cut out. For each cover cut three pattern pieces. Cut a 3" x 8" piece of fabric for a belt hanger/strap holder.

2. Pin the beaded trim along the seam line of the right side of one pattern piece, with the beads facing the center. Stitch the trim in place.

3. Remove the point from another pattern piece to make the cover front; fold under the raw edge and top-stitch.

4. With the right sides facing, pin and stitch the front to the back; trim the selvage and turn right-side-out.

5. For the lining, fold under the raw edges of the pointed flap of the remaining pattern piece and hand sew along beaded back flap. Trim and insert the length of the lining into the holder.

6. Fold the belt hanger/strap holder strip in half with right sides facing and sew the ends together to make a circle. Fold under the side raw edges and flatten out the circle. Insert the ends of the cord into one end and top-stitch along the long sides, securing the cording. Hand sew the hanger to the back of the cover along the short sides, top, and bottom.

7. Embellish the front of each cell phone holder as desired with tassels, beads and rhinestones.

· · · · · · · · · ·

Silhouette Lampshade

Make up some of these cheery lampshades, then turn on the light to watch the silhouettes come alive.

Supplies for 1 lampshade:

Vintage holiday artwork
for silhouettes
4 pieces transfer paper
Red bookbinding cloth
Small, sharp pointed
scissors
White cloth
lampshade
⅛" hole punch
White PVA
(bookbinding) glue
Foam brush for applying glue
Small brayer or roller
Pom-pom fringe or other desired trim

1. Gather your artwork and take it to your local copy shop to be copied onto transfer paper. They can also size the images up or down so all your images are in proportion, or out of proportion, whichever you wish.

2. Transfer the images to the paper backing of the bookbinding cloth, which is very sturdy and will stand up to cutting out intricate patterns without fraying.

3. On a cutting surface, cut out the silhouettes with small, sharp pointed scissors or a craft knife. With a craft knife, carefully cut out small details.

4. Lay the images on the lampshade to determine placement. Working quickly, with one shape at a time, brush PVA glue sparingly on the wrong side of the silhouette using a foam brush.

5. Position each shape on the lampshade as desired and roll over the shape firmly with brayer to be sure the edges are completely sealed. If not, slip a small piece of cardboard coated with PVA under any loose edges and roll again. Repeat with each silhouette.

6. Cut small circles for snowflakes from scraps of bookbinding cloth (you can use a ⅛" hole-punch for this) and glue these on the shade as shown.

7. Add pom-pom fringe to the bottom of the lampshade with craft glue or stitch it in place with a needle and matching thread.

■ HAVE A CHRISTMAS POLKA

If you want to decorate a ceramic lamp base with polka dots, choose a glass paint such as Ceramcoat. Clean the base according to the directions on the paint can. Add dots by dipping the handle of a foam brush in paint and dabbing on the lamp. To match the shades, we chose a red and white palette for the lamps; you might want to have darker shades that reflect a starry night sky, or a more traditional green and red combination.

Jacob's Ladder Calendar

Personalize a calendar that flips between months. This project gets easier as you go along; it's also a good one for groups to make assembly-line style.

Supplies for 1 calendar

Pre-printed calendar pages

Sobo glue

8½ yards black and white checked ribbon ⅜" wide

8 yards black and white checked ribbon ³/₁₆" wide

Six 10" x 12" pieces ³/₁₆"-thick black foam-core

Color photocopies of vintage illustrations

Extra-strength glue stick

Extra-long straight pins

White acrylic paint

Small-handled paintbrush or stylus

1. You can create your own monthly calendar page on the computer: make a grid and choose fancy fonts for the months, days, and dates. If you prefer, make a plain grid with pen and ink, have it copied at the copy shop, then cut out letters from magazines to spell out the names of the months and days and glue on with the glue stick.

2. Glue the ³/₁₆" ribbon along the edge of each piece of foam-core. Overlap the ribbon slightly where it meets.

3. Glue the calendar pages to the foam-core in the following manner: January through June will be on one side of the six panels and July through December on the reverse (January and July will share one board, February and August, March and September, etc.) The reverse sides must be upside down so that when the calendar flips, each month will be facing in the right direction.

4. Size the illustrations to fit above each calendar grid. Decorate each month with cut out illustrations, securing with the glue stick.

5. Construct the jacob's ladder from the calendar panels using four 8¼-yard lengths of ⅜" ribbon. To start, lay the pieces out end-to-end, in order, on the floor. Begin with January, fold over the end of a length of ribbon by about ⅛" and glue this folded end to the top edge of the foam-core, about ¼" in from the top left edge. Insert 2 long pins through the ribbon into the edge of the foam-core. Cover the heads of pins with a bit of glue to prevent the pins from pulling through the ribbon and to keep the ribbon from fraying. Repeat with another ribbon on the right side.

6. Bring these ribbons down the front of January and attach to the top of the February panel with pins and glue, butting the edges of the foam-core. Pass the ribbons behind the February panel and attach to the top edge of the March panel in same manner. Bring the ribbons down the front of March but behind April. Attach at the top of April, threading behind the April panel, and attach at the top of May.

7. Complete May and June as above, ending with a final attachment at the top of June. Fold the ribbon ends under ⅛" before inserting the pins.

8. Attach the ends of the 2 other lengths of ribbon to the bottom edge of the January panel, just to the inside of the initial lengths of ribbon, turning the edges under ⅛" and securing with pins and glue as above.

9. Bring the ribbons down the front of the February panel and secure at the bottom, then thread behind March, again securing at the bottom of March. Continue in the same way, ending by bringing the ribbons down the front of June and securing at the bottom edge.

10. Open the calendar. Holding January at the top of all the panels, fold the January panel down toward you. Each panel will flip accordingly. Turn the January panel the opposite way and the panels will flip again.

Painted Floorcloth

We say "Joy" but Believe, Hope, and Peace are all beautiful words. A piece of slipguard under the floorcloth will prevent slipping.

Supplies for 1 floorcloth

    Painted floorcloth template, pages 136, 137
    25" x 37" heavy cotton canvas
    Sobo glue
    8 to 12 ounces gesso
    Acrylic craft paint in large containers (black, dark green, light green, red, white, golden yellow) and small amounts of light blue and pink
    Paintbrushes
    Heavy paper for pattern
    Foam brush for glue
    Brayer or other roller
    Masking tape
    Yardstick
    Heavy-duty scissors
    Clear polyurethane spray

1. Press the canvas flat with a warm iron. With a ruler, mark a 1" hem all around in pencil. With the canvas face down, turn the edges over to meet the penciled line, mitering the corners. Press again with the iron.

2. Cover the inside of the hem with an even layer of Sobo glue and press firmly, rolling along the hem to flatten the crease and remove any excess glue. You may want to stitch the hem down.

3. Turn the canvas face up and prime with 2 coats of gesso. Let each coat dry well and sand lightly.

4. Mark and tape off a 1½" border all around the canvas with a pencil and ruler. Paint the border with 2 coats of white paint. Measure and lightly mark 1½" spacing for red checks. Paint the red checks along all 4 edges.

5. Enlarge the template for the center area of the floorcloth onto heavy paper and cut out. Tape the pattern to the canvas and trace carefully around the edge.

6. Mark and tape off a ½" border along the inside of the center shape. Paint it white. Mark and paint black squares evenly along the border. Paint small black dots at the center of each white square.

7. Paint the outside background with 2 coats of green paint and the center area with 2 coats of black paint.

8. Enlarge the letters from the pattern, cut them out, and trace onto the canvas. Paint the letters yellow.

9. Add small black dots to the green background by dipping the end of a paintbrush or a pencil eraser in black paint and dabbing on the dots. Add small white dots to the black background in the same way.

10. Enlarge the flowers from the pattern and trace onto canvas. Outline the flowers with black paint marker. Paint the centers as shown in the photograph on page 19. Add small white highlights close to the edge of each flower.

11. Liberally spray the floorcloth with several coats of polyurethane, letting each coat dry well.

Santa's Workshop

It's fun to date handmade projects. Then you can compare crafts from year to year and keep a collection of all the little variations. As your children grow, you'll see their artistry develop; many years down the line, when they have families of their own, you can make them a gift of their collection. How precious!

Peace Pillow

Show your patriotic stripes by making this peaceful pillow. In a pinch, this could even be made without a sewing machine.

Supplies for 1 pillow

- ¾ yard ticking fabric
- 1 yard white lining fabric
- ½ yard white cotton
- Small round bolster pillow, 15" long, 18" in diameter
- 15" white Velcro sew-on tape, ⅚" wide
- Aleene's Quick-Tac Glue
- ½ yard red cording
- 11 small green pom-poms for the ends of letters
- 1 yard ribbon

1. Measure and cut out 2 pieces of ticking, each 9¾" x 19½", and 1 white center panel, 12½" x 19½". These measurements include a seam allowance of ¼".

2. Sew the 2 striped side panels to the white panel along the long, 19" edges; press the seams flat at the back.

3. Cut a piece of lining fabric the same size as the front piece. With the right sides facing, stitch ½" from the edge all around, leaving a small opening on one side for turning. Turn right-side-out. Press and slip-stitch the opening closed.

4. Press the pillow to flatten the fabric, then top-stitch very close to the edge all along the edges and across the seam line on the ticking fabric.

5. Sew 15" lengths of Velcro tape to the center edges of the pillow fabric, 1 strip on the lining and 1 on the top fabric. The strips will overlap the ticking by several inches on each side.

6. Cut the cording to form letters. Stitch or glue the cording to the white fabric. Finish the ends of the letters with glued-on pom-poms.

7. Roll the bolster up in the fabric, securing with the Velcro closure. Tie each end of the bolster with ribbon.

Scottie Tea Cozy

A tea cozy is just what it says it is: a little insulated jacket for your teapot.

Supplies for 1 cozy

Scottie pattern, page 138
8" x 8" piece black felt
3" x 3" piece red felt
¾ yard red and white
    fabric with large
    polka dots
¾ yard thin batting
¼ yard fusible bonding
    material
¾ yard small red and
    white polka dot fabric
Tiny white button

1. Following the patterns, create a scottie appliqué by cutting a dog and collar from felt. Iron fusible bonding to the back of each appliqué following the bonding instructions.

2. Make a small red fabric loop by cutting a strip of polka-dot fabric 1½" x 5". Fold in ¼" on each wrong side. Fold in half. Top-stitch closed.

3. Cut out the dot fabric, lining, and batting from the template, adding ¼" seam allowance on all sides. Stitch the lining and batting together with the right sides facing. Clip the seam and stitch the lining ⅛" smaller all around.

4. Iron the scottie appliqué to the center front. Machine stitch all around ⅛" from the edge.

5. With the right sides facing, and the loop placed at the top facing down and in, stitch the front and back of the tea cozy together. Turn right-side-out. Baste a ¼" hem at the bottom of the cozy.

6. Insert the lining, with batting attached, with the wrong sides together. Turn under ¼" all along the bottom. Hem to the outside fabric.

7. Sew on a little white button for the dog's eye.

Gingerbread Village

Break the village down into simple steps and have fun making it. This one's not really for eating, just admiring.

Supplies for 1 village

Village templates,
    pages 140, 141

GINGERBREAD
½ cup brown sugar
¼ cup shortening
¾ cup molasses
⅓ cup water
3½ cups flour
1 teaspoon baking soda
1 teaspoon ground ginger
½ teaspoon allspice
½ teaspoon ground cinnamon
½ teaspoon ground cloves
½ teaspoon salt

ROYAL ICING
8 cups confectioners' sugar
1½ tablespoons cream of tartar
1¼ cups egg whites
Blue, red, green, and yellow food coloring

Red pipe cleaners
2 ounces prepared marzipan

1. Preheat the oven to 350°F. Grease 2 baking sheets.

2. In the large bowl of an electric mixer, cream the sugar and shortening on medium speed until light and fluffy. Add the molasses and mix until combined. Stir in the cold water just until combined.

3. In another large bowl, sift the flour, baking soda, ginger, allspice, cinnamon, cloves, and salt. Stir into the wet ingredients just until combined. Shape the dough into a ball, cover with plastic wrap, and chill.

4. Roll the dough out to a ⅛"-thickness. Using the templates, cut the dough into desired shapes. Transfer

(continued on next page)

the dough to the prepared baking sheets. Bake the gingerbread for 15 minutes, or until firm to the touch. Transfer to wire racks and let cool completely.

5. Make the royal icing: In the large bowl of an electric mixer fitted with the paddle attachment, combine the confectioners' sugar with the cream of tartar. Mix on low speed and add the egg whites. Continue mixing for 5 minutes, or until smooth. Cover the bowl with a damp cloth while you are preparing the colors.

6. Divide the icing into small bowls or teacups. Tint the icing to desired colors, keeping 2 bowls white. You will need 2 consistencies of each icing; 1 stiff and 1 thin. Thick icings should be stiff enough to hold soft peaks when lifted with a spoon; thin icing should be like buttermilk. Adjust the consistency by adding confectioners' sugar or a few drops of water. Keep each bowl of icing covered while you are working.

7. Decorate the houses: Spoon the thick icings into individual pastry bags, each bag fitted with a small round tip. With the white icing, outline the snowy roofs.

8. With the thick consistency of the white or colored icing, outline the other parts of the buildings: doors, windows, roofs, chimneys. Let the gingerbread sit for 10 minutes, or until the icing is completely dry.

9. With the thin icings, fill all the areas with matching colors, easing the icing with the bowl of a small spoon. The icing can be coaxed with a toothpick. Do not disturb the outlines. Allow the cookies to dry flat at room temperature overnight.

10. Once the icing is completely dried, add all the details you like, such as doorknobs, trim, shutters, house numbers, and welcome signs.

11. Make chimney smoke: Cut the pipe cleaners into 3" lengths and bend. Pipe a large button of icing onto the back of the chimney and place the end of the pipe cleaner into the middle. Hold for 2 minutes.

12. Make the school sign: Roll the marzipan to a ⅛"-thick rectangle. Trim the edges straight using a ruler. Write the word "school" with a toothpick and dye.

Votive Candle Holders

Wherever you make these, prepare the area with lots of newspaper, so that the spray glue and glitter can be quickly cleaned away once you've finished the candleholders. Silver or gold glitter would work too.

Supplies for 2 candleholders

Musical notes to photocopy

¼ yard clear contact paper

Newspapers, for work surface

One 12" glass vase

One 8" glass vase

Spray glue

1 large container matte white glitter

2 white votive candles

1. Enlarge 2 musical notes with a photocopier to a size that looks pleasing on the sides of the vases.

2. With a craft knife, cut out the photocopied notes to use as patterns. Place the patterns on clear contact paper, trace, and cut out.

3. Adhere a contact paper note, centered, on a vase. Working on newspaper, spray glue all over the vase sides. Sprinkle glitter all over the glued area. Repeat the process with the second vase.

4. Let the glitter dry. Remove the contact-paper notes.

5. Place a small bit of water in the bottom of each vase, and add a votive candle. Water automatically puts the candle out when it burns down—a good safety tip.

Christmas Tree Tackboard

Slip Christmas cards under the rick-rack garlands of the tree; this is one to keep and bring out every year.

To make the tree

- 24" x 18" foam-core board, ½" thick
- 24" x 18" corrugated backing board
- 4 yards green and white checked fabric
- 1 yard thin fleece or batting
- 4½ yards red rick-rack
- Craft knife, ruler and cutting surface
- Craft glue and foam brush
- Masking tape
- Straight pins
- Wire cutter
- ¼ yard red felt
- Red cotton thread
- 3 graduated sizes of buttons
- 12" decorative ribbon trim, ½" wide

1. Cut a tree shape with a trunk from foam-core. Cut a matching shape from the corrugated backing board.

2. Place the tree shape on the checked fabric and cut around it, leaving a generous allowance of fabric that can be turned under the edges.

3. Lightly brush glue on the face of the foam-core tree, then place the glued side on the fleece. Trim the fleece even with edges of the tree.

4. Align the checked fabric on the fleece face of the tree and turn the edges under, securing with masking tape on the reverse side. Clip the corners and points of fabric as needed to cover the tree branches. Glue the fabric to hold the clipped edges in place.

5. For the back, cover the corrugated tree shape with checked fabric, turning and securing the fabric edges with masking tape.

6. Add rick-rack trim to the front of the tree to create a garland. Secure the rick-rack with masking tape.

7. Apply craft glue liberally to the back of the tree and place the corrugated tree and foam-core tree back to back. Place the tree on a flat surface and add some weight—a few books will do—until the tree is fully dry.

8. Clip the straight pins with wire cutter to ½" length. With a dot of glue on each, push the pins securely into each intersection of rick-rack. Cover each pinhead with a button secured with a generous dab of glue.

9. Cut 2 trunk-shaped pieces from red felt. Join the pieces with a blanket stitch along the sides and bottom with red perle cotton.

10. Apply glue to the back of the trunk and gently ease it into the top of the pot. Glue ribbon trim along the rim of the pot and glue a large bow or an ornament to the top of the tree.

11. Add a hanger to the back of the tackboard: knot a 6" piece of rick-rack. Hot-glue or staple the rick-rack to the back, near the top.

White Mouse Ornament

If you're going to make a mouse, make a bunch of them; they're so adorable everyone will want one.

Supplies for 1 mouse

Mouse pattern, page 139

12" square clear contact paper

8" square white felt

1 white pipe cleaner

Cotton batting

Aleene's Quik-Dry tacking glue

8" square red felt

Black, white, and red embroidery thread

Tiny black pom-pom

Blusher make-up

1. Trace the patterns onto clear contact paper and cut out. Double over the white felt, and cut out 2 pieces. With a running stitch, sew an outline in white thread around the mouse close to the edge of the pattern. Trim ¹⁄₁₆" from the stitch line.

2. On the mouse's back, make a ¾" slit. Insert white pipe cleaners into the arms and legs, and add a bit of stuffing to round out the head and body. Slip-stitch the opening closed.

3. Cut out and glue on the ears, bringing the cut area together to round out the shape.

4. Cut out the robe from red felt and stitch along the sides and shoulders. Cut out a small triangle of felt from the top front of the robe, then cut a slit from the point of the triangle to the bottom. Cut a small strip of felt for a collar. Put the robe on the mouse, then glue the collar to the robe. Tie the robe closed with embroidery thread.

5. Add details to the mouse's face. Embroider the eyes and mouth with a small plain stitch. Glue on a pom-pom nose. With a fingertip, dot blusher on the cheek and ears.

6. Cut a tail piece following the pattern. Glue the squared end to the back of the robe.

Tree Gift Box Ornament

Here's an idea that can work on any shape cardboard box, though we are fond of Christmas trees. If you decide on a square or rectangular box, you could save time by covering it with a sturdy giftwrap, rather than acrylic paint.

Supplies for 1 box

Medium-size foam brush

1 tree-shape paper box, 5½" tall

Small bottles of white and red acrylic paint

Fine-point paintbrush

Santa illustration

Sobo glue

Small self-adhesive red paper dots

Buttons

Ribbon

1. With the foam brush, paint the box inside and out with white paint. Let dry.

2. With a ruler and pencil mark narrow vertical red stripes on the lid. Fill in the stripes with red paint using a fine-point brush. Let the paint dry completely.

3. Cut out the Santa art and brush Sobo glue evenly onto the back. Glue to the lid.

4. Add red dots in alternating rows between the stripes.

5. Attach decorative buttons with a glue gun. On the top of the box, near the edge, hot-glue the ends of two 8" lengths of ribbon for hanging, then replace the lid. Tie the other ends of the ribbon in a small bow.

Vintage Holiday Fabric Placemat

Salvage vintage tablecloths to make a set of reversible holiday placemats. For a fancy dinner set, replace the rick-rack with frilly lace.

Supplies for 4 placemats

- 2 vintage holiday tablecloths
- Coordinating holiday print fabric for the border
- Four 15" x 22" pieces thin cotton batting
- 8½ yards giant red rick-rack trim

1. Cut four 15" x 22" front pieces from the tablecloth, choosing matching designs of fabric, if possible. Cut 4 back panels from a coordinating fabric in the same size.

2. Sandwich quilt batting between the wrong sides of the front and back pieces; pin in position.

3. Cut 4"-wide strips of border fabric to fit around the placemat. Fold and press the strips in half lengthwise. Fold under the raw edges ¼" and press.

4. To attach the borders, open 1 side strip and place it against a short side edge of the back of the mat, with right sides facing. Pin and stitch in place. Fold the border strip over to the front of the mat and press. Cut rick-rack to fit, position it just under the folded edge of the border strip, and pin in place. Stitch along the front edge of the fold of the border strip.

5. Repeat for the other short side strips, then for each of the longer sides, overlapping the strips at the corners. Fold under the raw ends of the long strips, aligning the folds with the edges of the side strips.

6. Slip-stitch the ends of the folded border strips closed.

Vintage Holiday Fabric Chair Pad

Make chair pads to enhance your holiday dining room. Spray starch will make them nice and crisp.

Supplies for 4 chair pads

- 1 vintage holiday tablecloth
- ½ yard cotton quilt batting
- ½ yard white fabric for backing
- ½ yard coordinating polka dot or print fabric for ruffle
- 2 yards red seam binding
- Ribbon

1. Measure the chair seats and make a paper pattern to size. Use the pattern to cut 8 matching sections from the tablecloth, taking the best advantage of the pattern and adding ½" seam allowance all around.

2. Sandwich the seat fabrics together, right sides facing up and the batting in between the 2 layers. Pin to hold the pieces in place. Top-stitch close to the edge.

3. Cut the ruffle fabric into long 4" strips. Sew the ends of several strips together until you have enough ruffle to go 1½ times around the chair pad. Pleat the strip with ½" pleats every 3 inches and pin the pleats in place. Baste along the pleated raw edge to secure.

4. Turn the other long raw edge of the ruffle under ¼", then turn under again to make a neat hem. Press and top-stitch close to the edge.

5. Pin and machine zig-zag stitch the ruffles raw edge to the chair pad edges. Trim the excess ruffle. Stitch the remaining raw ends together to join the ruffle.

6. Pin and stitch seam binding around the raw edges of the chair pad, with the binding open and raw edges and right sides facing. Fold the binding over the edges and pin in place. Top-stitch through all the layers all along the edge to secure.

7. Stitch ribbon ties to the back corners of the seat pads.

Snow Family Topiary

Here's a gift that not only lasts from year to year, it becomes more meaningful each Christmas as children grow.

Supplies for the snow family

- 4 larger Styrofoam balls
- 4 smaller Styrofoam balls
- Glaze-Tex All White Christmas Drape
- Black plastic-headed straight pins
- 2 small black buttons
- Small saw
- One ¼"-width wooden dowel
- Carving knife
- Rich Art paint in poster white, brilliant red and yellow-orange
- Smooth white cardstock
- Clear glitter
- Stapler

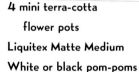

- 4 mini terra-cotta flower pots
- Liquitex Matte Medium
- White or black pom-poms
- Large and small paper cups
- Accessories: pearls, bow ties, eyeglasses

1. With a craft knife, hollow an indent at the base of each Styrofoam ball. Cut 2 circles of Christmas Drape large enough to cover each ball.

2. Gather the 2 layers of Drape around a ball, forming pleats, and hot-glue the edges in the flattened area at the bottom of the ball. Repeat for each ball.

3. Use black-headed pins to make the mouth. For eyes, attach the buttons with a hot-glue gun.

4. With a saw, cut the wooden dowel into small pieces for the noses. Shape each with a carving knife. Make both ends sharp so that a pointed end can be inserted into the ball. Paint the noses orange. When they are completely dry, insert a nose in each face.

5. For the cardstock collar: Use a circle template or compass to draw a circle the same size as the neck of the figure. Draw another circle about ¾" larger. Cut out along the inner and outer guides, giving the outer circle a decorative edge. Paint the collar white and trim with glitter.

6. Cut out a ½" pie-shaped wedge from the collar. Pull the edges together and staple them to close.

7. Glue the larger ball to the bottom of the collar with hot-glue; then glue the smaller ball on top.

8. To make the hats, seal the little flower pots with 1 coat of the matte medium and let dry for an hour. Paint the pots white; let dry completely. Using a circle template, trace the polka-dots and paint with red paint. Adhere the hat to the top of the head with hot-glue. You could also make hats from cardboard with ribbon trim.

9. Glue on pom-poms for ears.

10. Paint the edge of 4 paper cups red and then paint dots in various sizes on the outside of the cups. Write each person's name with a felt marker. Add a bit of glue to the inner rim of each cup before inserting the snow figures. Place the snow figures in the cups, weighting them with dried beans if necessary.

 # Santa's Workshop

Once the season is here, you'll be looking for the same tools and supplies time and again. You need Santa's Toolbox! A red plastic toolbox with a hinged lid, the kind you'll find at the hardware store, can keep all your glitters and glues and brushes together. Just toss it in the car for church or community decorating projects.

Patchwork Mitten Bandboxes

Découpage is a technique that's always in style; choose stripes and checks or a combination of holiday patterns.

Supplies for 1 set of boxes

- 3 cardboard mitten-shaped nesting boxes
- Acrylic craft paint in ivory and desired background colors
- Assorted letter rubber stamps and green ink pad
  or paper printed with words
- Découpage medium
- Assorted art/craft paper
- Black paint pen
- Medium-size foam brush
- Sobo glue
- Clear glitter
- 24" white cotton ball fringe
- 1/2 yard red and white checked ribbon
- 1 medium-size button

1. Paint the inside and bottom of each box with 2 coats of acrylic paint. Let the boxes dry between coats. Paint the mitten cuffs with 2 coats of ivory paint. Let the boxes dry between coats.

2. To personalize the boxes, rubber stamp the desired words on artpaper.

3. Cut small pieces of paper in a variety of shapes and position them on the lid, working out from the words in a patchwork pattern. Rework the pieces to complete a pleasing design. Use the découpage medium and a brush to adhere the papers on the lid of the box.

4. To the sides of the box, apply a patchwork of paper pieces that match the design on the top.

5. Cover the whole box with several layers of découpage medium, following the directions on the container. Let the medium dry between coats.

6. When dry, add stitch lines to outline each paper "patch" using the black paint marker.

7. Paint the cuff with diluted white glue; sprinkle generously with glitter. Let the glue dry completely and shake off the loose glitter.

8. On the 2 larger boxes, glue ball fringe where the cuff meets the pattern. On the smallest box, tie a length of ribbon into a festive bow. Glue the bow and a button to the top edge of the cuff.

■ THREE THUMBS UP!

We designed the nesting boxes for food: one says "Nuts to You," the second, "Sweets for the Sweet," and the smallest is "Sugarplums." You could personalize the boxes with names or customize them for art supplies.

Make-Up Bag

Grab your remnant box and go to town! These darling storage bags justify all the bits and pieces of beautiful fabric you've been collecting all year.

Supplies for 1 make-up bag

1 yard polka-dot fabric

½ yard cotton batting

¾ yard Christmas-pattern fabric

Scraps of polka-dot cotton and gingham

2 yards striped piping

4 red Velcro sew-on circles

1 white Velcro sew-on circle

Four 1½" green buttons

1 larger red button

1. Measure and cut out the lining, outer fabric, and batting; each piece is 13½" x 19". Hand baste the batting to the lining, easing the stitches to lie flat.

2. Measure and cut 2 pieces of fabric for each pocket. There are a total of 5 pockets: one, 19" x 5¼"; one, 5½" x 7½"; three 7½" x 5¼".

3. With right sides facing, stitch the pocket pieces all around the edge, leaving an opening to turn. Turn the fabric to the right side. Press with a warm iron. Slip-stitch the opening closed.

4. Fold the fabric up to form a 9" long pocket with a 2¼" flap at the top. Top-stitch the top flap close to the edge.

Baste the pocket to the right side of the lining of the case and top-stitch in position. Sew Velcro circles under the flap and on the pocket to close. Finish with a decorative button on the outside of the flap; for color, we sewed the green buttons on with red thread.

5. Make the small pockets. With right sides facing, stitch along the edges, leaving an opening to turn. Turn to the right side, press and slip-stitch closed. Fold up from the bottom, leaving 1½" for the flap. Baste the pockets to the lining of case, then top-stitch them in position. Sew on Velcro circles, and add a button to each flap.

6. Make the brush holder. With right sides facing, sew together at the edges, leaving an opening to turn. Turn to the right side and slip-stitch the opening closed. Pin to the left side of the lining and top-stitch in place along the sides and bottom. Top-stitch three parallel seams to create small pockets to hold brushes.

7. With the piping facing down toward the center of the fabric, sew the piping to the edges of the lining fabric. With the right sides facing, sew the lining and outside case fabrics together, leave a 6" opening to turn. Turn to the right side and slip-stitch the opening closed. Fold the case in thirds, adding Velcro circles.

8. Sew a button on the center front of the case.

■ HIT THE ROAD, JACK

Customize the bag for a man by adapting the brush holder to accommodate a razor, a comb, toothbrush, and toothpaste. The three small pockets can hold cuff links, change, and spare keys. The longer pocket is fine for a tie. Of course, you'll choose some manly fabrics.

Wine Gift Bag

A bottle of cheer, especially a homemade flavored vodka, is that much cheerier in a custom gift sack. Rich fabrics like velvet and linen damask make the bags sophisticated and luxurious. No special sewing skills are required.

Supplies for 1 wine bag

- 13" x 18" holly-pattern lining fabric
- 13" x 18" green-and-white-check fabric
- ½ yard cording at least ½" thick
- Sobo glue
- Two 3" tassels

1. With the right sides facing, fold the check fabric in half lengthwise and stitch the long side ¼" in from the edge, leaving the top and bottom open. Repeat with the lining fabric, adding ⅛" to the seam allowance to make the lining slightly smaller than the outer bag.

2. With the right sides of the bag facing out and the right side of the lining facing inward, slide the lining into the bag. Align the center seams at the back of the bag.

3. Baste the bottom seam close the edge. Turn the bag to the right side and top-stitch along the bottom seam ¼" from the edge. Turn the bag to the right side. Turn in the upper edge ¼" on both the lining and the outer bag. Baste and top-stitch closed.

4. At the bottom of the bag, gather the 2 end points and bring them together to the center so the bottom lies flat. Hand-stitch and press.

5. Glue the ends of the cording with Sobo glue so that they don't unravel. When the glue is dry, sew one cord end securely to a tassel top. Repeat for the other end. Tie around the gift bag.

■ HOW TO GET SACKED

Gift bags are handy for presents that don't take easily to conventional boxes—basketballs, baby toys, flashlights. If you visit during the holidays, make a giant sack to hold all the presents for each family.

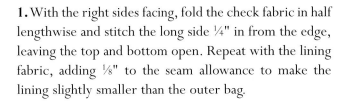

Santa's Workshop

Copper wire is an all-purpose Christmas fixer. Out of ribbon? Tie gifts with copper wire. Have an ornament without a hook? Copper wire looks better than a paper clip! Random pillar candles? Round them up and hold them together with copper wire. Hang your greeting cards over wire stretched across a doorway or entry.

Welcome Home Garland

Our gingerbread village was so popular that we decided to adapt it to more permanent materials. Voilà—the Welcome Home Garland! Virtually weightless foam-core board replaces the gingerbread, and you can create as much detail as you like from paper, paint, ribbon.

Supplies for 1 garland

House templates,
    page 140-141
³⁄₁₆" foam-core
    board
Art/craft papers
    in a variety of
    colors, weights,
    and patterns
Masking tape
Rick-rack, buttons,
    and other trims
White cardstock
Clear mailing tape
Fine-tip black marker
Tacky craft glue
Foam brush
1 yard check ribbon

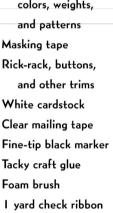

1. Trace the template onto heavy paper and cut out a pattern. Trace houses and roof shapes on foam-core and cut out using a sharp craft knife.

2. Cover each house with the desired background paper. Brush the back of the paper with glue and smooth down on the foam-core, wrapping the edges around to the back. Secure with masking tape and trim the edges. If you wish, cover the back of the house with paper.

3. Cut roof shapes from colored paper and glue on. Glue rick-rack trim around the roof edge. For a flat roof with dormer, cut shingles from paper and edge each shingle with a marker. Glue on shingles in alternating layers.

4. Create window trim from white cardstock with cut-out window shapes. Make window panes underneath by covering yellow paper with clear mailing tape, to make shiny panes. Glue the windows on the houses.

5. To make shutters that open, cut 2 shapes from the same paper, leaving small tabs on one long side of each piece. Fold the tabs to the back. Attach the shutters by gluing the tab at the side of the window.

6. Glue on button doorknobs and any other trim you would like including rick-rack along the edge of the roof line and bits of cording for door hinges.

7. With a fine-tip marker, write a welcome on cardstock. Add trim to the edges and attach to the house.

8. To make the houses into a garland, attach one end of checked ribbon to the back of a house just below the roofline with tacky glue. Add more houses to the garland in the same manner.

Holly Leaf Garland

Finally those metal shop classes will pay off! The heavy foil in the holly garland will help keep the leaf shape, both while it's on display and later, when it's stored away. You'll change the look of the garland entirely by using foil in just one color. If you have an awkward space or one that is hard to decorate, customize the size of the garland.

Supplies for 1 garland

Holly leaf pattern, page 139

6" piece lightweight cardboard

1 roll each heavy red, green, silver, and gold foil

Wire cutters and scissors

Spool of 18-gauge copper wire

1 bunch of wired red berries

1. Transfer the holly leaf pattern to cardboard and cut out. With a pencil, trace 16 or 18 leaves onto each color foil. Using sharp scissors, cut out each leaf.

2. Cut the paper pattern along the vein line, then trace a vein onto each foil with a dull pencil or a ball burnisher, if you have one. Bend one side of each leaf up to shape.

3. Cut two 24" lengths of copper wire. Place the stem end of one leaf on the stem end of another. Starting about 6" from the end of the wire, twist the leaf ends around the wire. Cut a 6" to 8" inch length of wire. Twist one end tightly around both the leaf ends and the wire. Wrap the other end around a pencil several times to coil it into a curly-vine shape.

4. Add 3 or 4 stems of berries after each leaf group, twisting each one around the wire to secure.

5. Continue adding berries, vines, and leaves, alternating the colors, down the length of the wire, leaving about 6" at the end to attach.

6. Adjust the leaves and berries as desired, and hang.

■ SILVER AND GOLD HOLLYDAYS

Decorate wrapped gifts with foil holly leaves. Punch a hole at the top center of each leaf and attach it to the package with a slip of copper wire.

TEMPLATES

Making Christmas crafts that come out perfect every time is easy with these templates as your guides! For easy use year after year, photocopy these onto transfer paper, label them, and file them away!

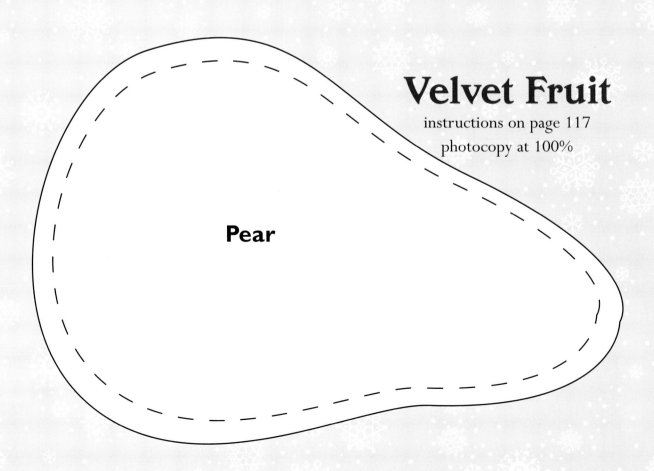

Velvet Fruit

instructions on page 117
photocopy at 100%

Pear

Velvet Fruit

instructions on page 117

photocopy at 100%

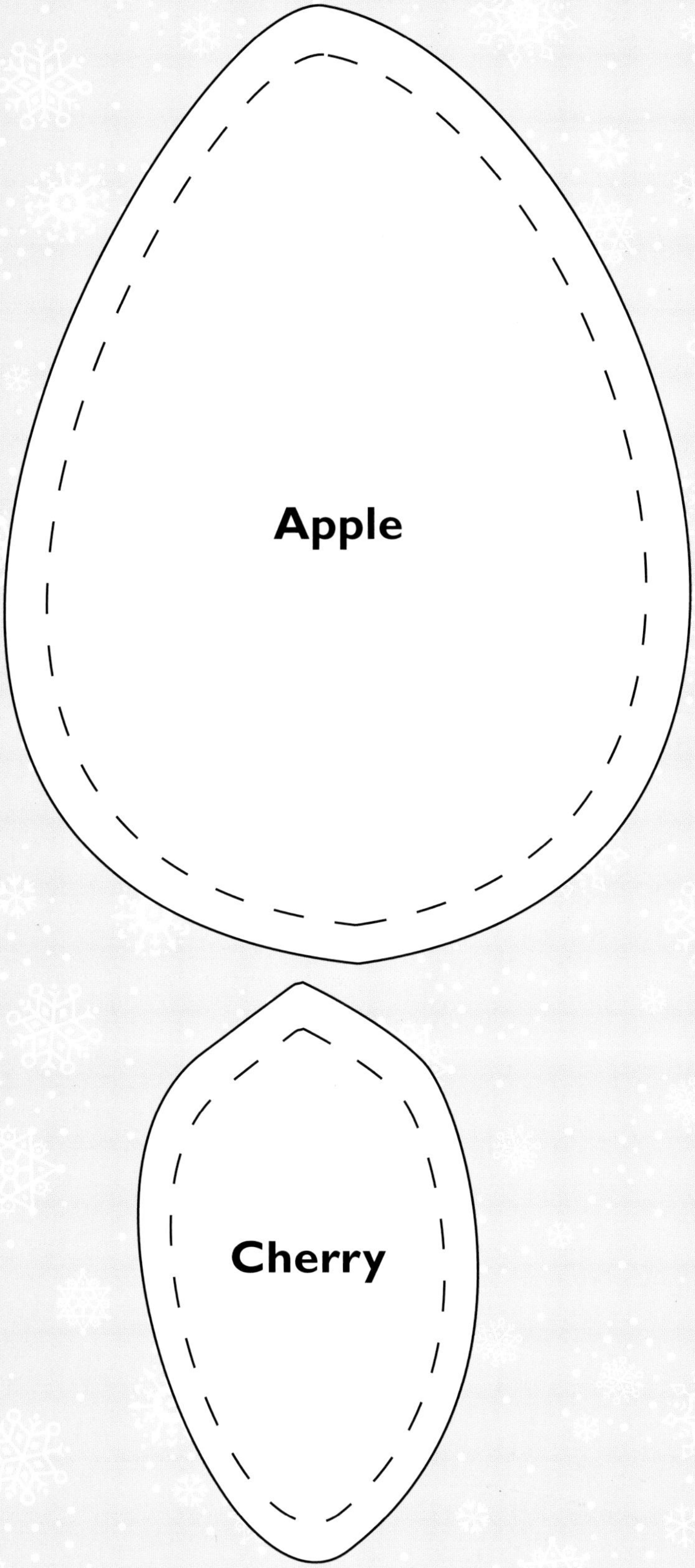

Apple

Cherry

Cell Phone Holder

instructions on page 118

photocopy at 100%

fold

Painted Floorcloth

instructions on page 121

photocopy at 200%
(each quadrant should be 14 inches long)

Scottie Tea Cozy

instructions on page 123

photocopy at 100%

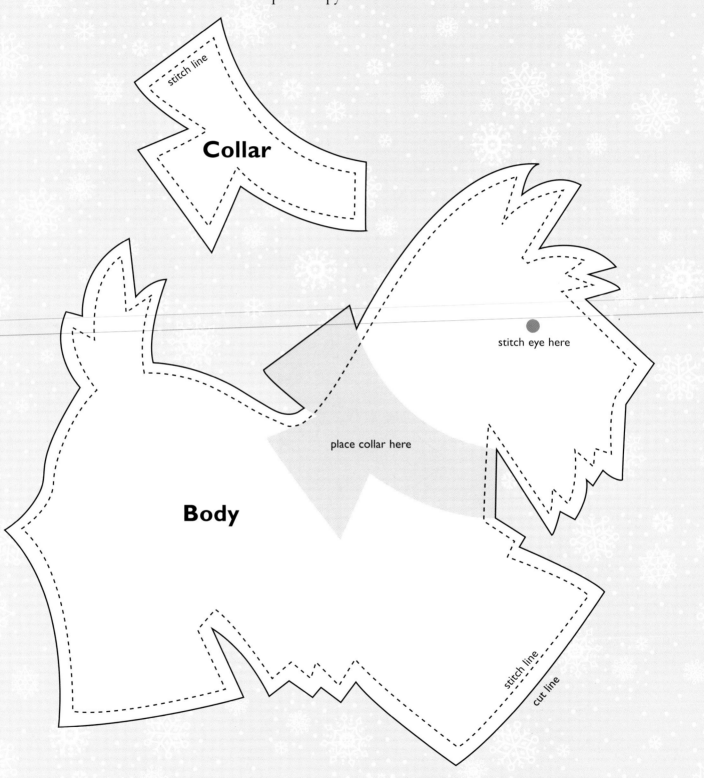

stitch line

Collar

stitch eye here

place collar here

Body

stitch line

cut line

Holly Leaf Garland

instructions on page 133

photocopy at 100%

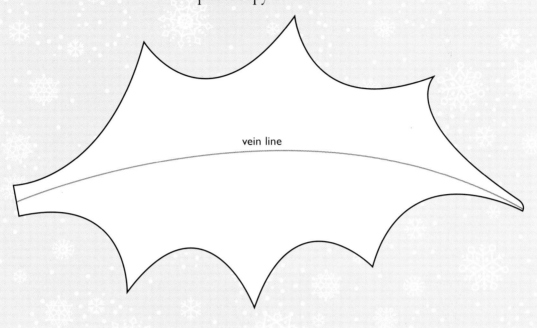

vein line

White Mouse Ornament

instructions on page 126

photocopy at 100%

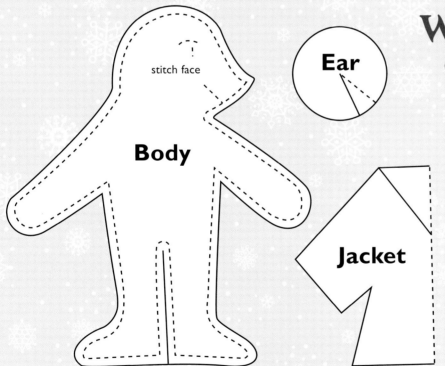

stitch face

Body

Ear

Jacket

Collar

Tail

Gingerbread Village

instructions on page 123

photocopy at 125%

House A

Church

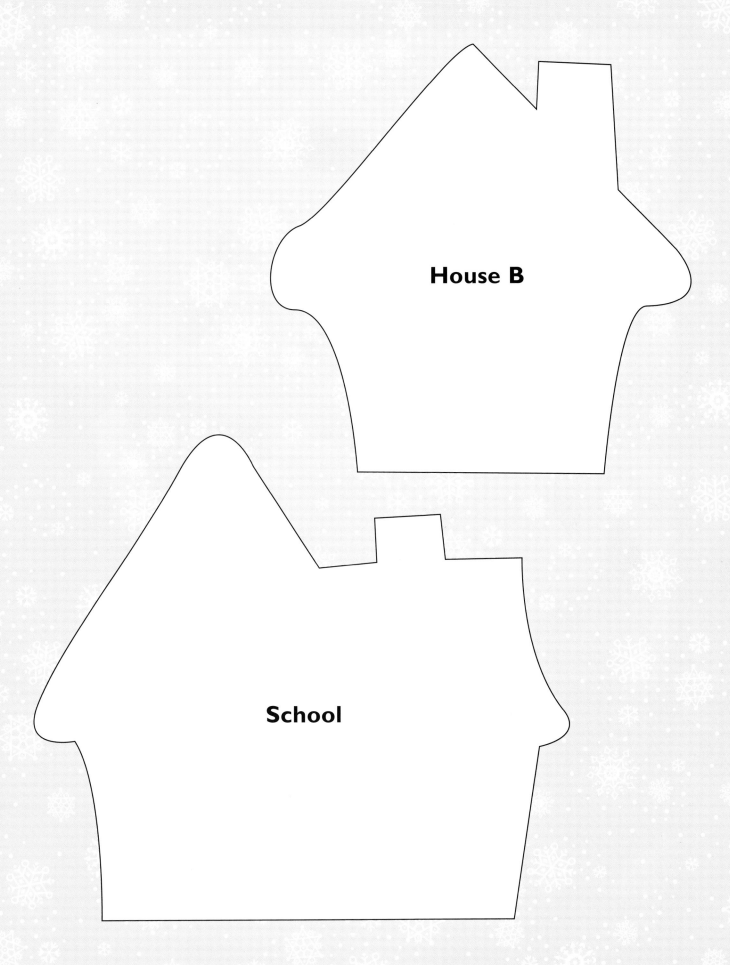

House B

School

Resources

Made at the North Pole
· · · · · · · · · ·

The Night Before Christmas
· · · · · · · · · ·

The More The Merrier
· · · · · · · · · ·